A walk in the yard

𝒜 𝓌𝒶𝓁

NAVAL INSTITUTE PRESS
ANNAPOLIS, MARYLAND

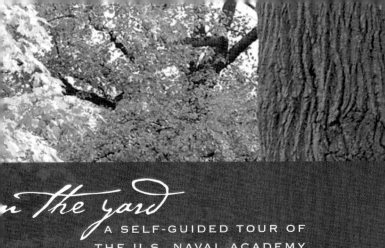

n the yard

A SELF-GUIDED TOUR OF
THE U.S. NAVAL ACADEMY

TAYLOR BALDWIN KILAND and JAMIE HOWREN

Naval Institute Press
291 Wood Road
Annapolis, MD 21402

Library of Congress Cataloging-in-Publication Data
Howren, Jamie, 1966–
  A walk in the yard : a self-guided walking tour of the U.S. Naval
Academy / Jamie Howren and Taylor Baldwin Kiland.
      p. cm.
  Includes bibliographical references and index.
  ISBN-13: 978-1-59114-436-6 (alk. paper)
  ISBN-10: 1-59114-436-1 (alk. paper)
  1. United States Naval Academy—Tours. 2. United States Naval
Academy—Maps, Tourist. I. Kiland, Taylor Baldwin, 1966– II.
Title.
V415.L3H68 2007 359.0071'173—dc22

                                                    2006033540

Interior designed by Tony Meisel
Printed in the United States of America on acid-free paper

25 24 23 22 21 20   12 11 10 9 8 7 6

To my daughter, Elle, with much love and pride.
—*Jamie*

To my Papa, Capt. Ingolf Norman Kiland Jr., Class of 1959, who instilled in me a love of country and a penchant for the Navy blue and gold, and to my beloved mother, Anne Harrington Kiland, who encouraged me to be a writer as soon as I could pick up a pen. And, of course, to the ghost of my grandfather, Vice Adm. Ingolf N. Kiland, Class of 1917, whose spirit guided me around the Yard.
—*Taylor*

Note to visitors: The Yard is an active military installation. Visitor access can change without notice, due to heightened security measures. In addition, building construction and renovations can necessitate the relocation of various collections, e.g., cannons, sculptures, historic flags, and artwork.

● This symbol, appearing throughout the book, indicates that this building is not open to the public on a regular basis.

Contents

Acknowledgments

We are grateful to Midn. Bert Bender, Rob Bender, Boggs & Partners, Lou Ann Broad, Dr. Jennifer Bryan, Vice Adm. and Mrs. Al Burkhalter, Capt. David Byerly, Judy Campbell, Mackie Christenson, Dr. Ed Cook, Jeannie Anderson Coppedge, Ed Cotter, CSD Architects, Tom Cutler, Kim Anderson Diana, Lt. Cdr. Rebecca Dickinson, Dan Eytchison, John Fleet, Cdr. Rob Gibbons, Deb Goode, Scott Harmon, Skid Heyworth, Bob Hofford, Jo Howren, Mianna Jopp, Chris Kidd, Rear Adm. Randy King, Gary LaValley, Rear Adm. Robert McNitt, Vice Adm. and Mrs. Hank Mustin, Cdr. John Mustin, Shannon O'Connor, John Quinn, Vice Adm. and Mrs. Rodney Rempt, Ian Richards, Dr. Mark Richards, Col. and Mrs. John Ripley, Hillary Schenker, Capt. Ned Shuman, Sigrid Trumpy, James Watt, Capt. Allison Webster-Giddings, John Wilson, Midn. Liz Yatko, and Jim Cheevers—Naval Academy historian whose passion for and knowledge of the Yard are unsurpassed.

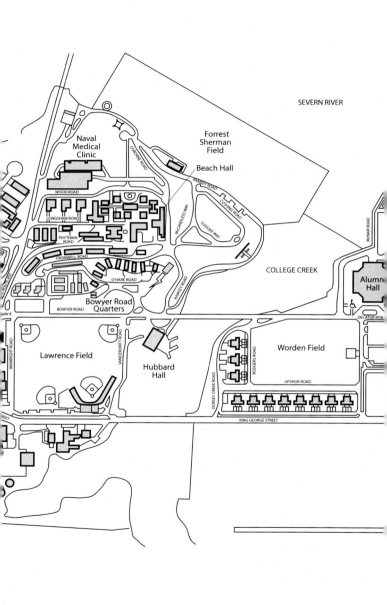

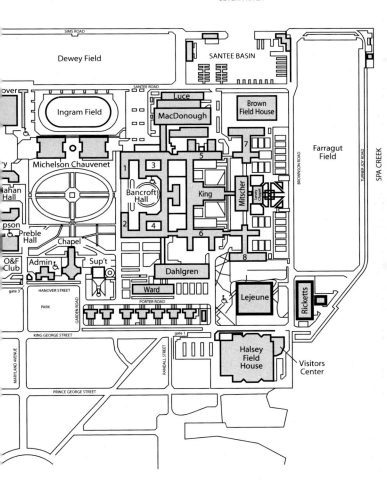

SEVERN RIVER

SIMS ROAD

Dewey Field

SANTEE BASIN

SANTEE ROAD

Ingram Field

Luce

MacDonough

Brown
Field House

Michelson Chauvenet

7

Farragut
Field

Bancroft
Hall

1

3

5

King

Mitscher

Lowry
Chapel

Mahan
Hall

mpson

2

4

6

Preble
Hall

Chapel

8

O&F
Club

Admin

Sup't

Dahlgren

Ward

Lejeune

Ricketts

gate 3'

HANOVER STREET

PARK

GARDEN ROAD

PORTER ROAD

KING GEORGE STREET

gate 1

Halsey
Field
House

Visitors
Center

MARYLAND AVENUE

RANDALL STREET

PRINCE GEORGE STREET

BROWNSON ROAD

TURNER JOY ROAD

SPA CREEK

A walk in the yard

An aerial view of the Naval Academy.
Photo © Alan Kachmacher. *Courtesy Boggs & Partners Architects*

Introduction

THE YARD

As a state capital, college town, sailing port, and tourist destination, Annapolis, Maryland, is a unique Mecca, a confluence of multiple cultural influences. The governor, the state legislature, famous sailors, and the "Johnnies" of St. John's College continue to leave their indelible marks on this historic city. Sequestered behind brick walls, however, lies another city within this city—the campus of the U.S. Naval Academy, or "the Yard," as it is commonly called.

Until visitors venture inside the Yard, they may not fully understand the legacies inherent in its buildings and monuments. The U.S. Naval Academy is a city of men and women who are dedicating four years of their lives to become leaders of our nation's Navy and Marine Corps. By walking inside the walls of the Yard, you can take a closer look at what and who inspires and motivates them. The people who teach them give words of encouragement. The stories behind the namesake buildings and monuments provide the heroic standards they seek to emulate.

Once you walk through the gates, you enter a historic, majestic, and almost mystical compound of structures,

DID YOU KNOW?
"The Yard": Where does the term originate? It dates back to the Revolutionary War and evolved from the term "dockyard," used to describe any naval installation. The campus of the U.S. Naval Academy has been officially called "the Yard" since the school was founded in 1845.

meticulously designed and steeped in tradition and history. A walk in the Yard can take hours or days, depending on the topic or your level of interest. Architectural buffs, military historians, and families with children all can find something appealing within its walls. Even a quick or a circuitous walk around the Yard can yield hidden treasures: the largest collections of Beaux-Arts architecture in the United States, antique cannons from the Spanish–American War, tombstones of heroes from World War II, a large collection of Currier and Ives prints, antique flags that flew on famous warships, and even the crypt of John Paul Jones, who died at the end of the eighteenth century.

The Yard and the institution it houses are inextricably linked. The students here, the Brigade of Midshipmen, become family for each other and the buildings their de facto home for four years. Remember how you felt at age eighteen, then imagine instead traveling far away and living among strangers, being abruptly denied the comforts of freedom and mobility, forced to learn new habits and trust new authorities—thrust into the world of Honor, Courage, Commitment above all else. Everywhere you turn within the walls of the Yard are physical reminders of others who have spent four years here, physical memorials to those

---

ENTERING THE YARD
While the Yard comprises a college campus, it also houses an active military installation. Military personnel must have a valid Department of Defense-issued car decal to drive onto the Yard. The Yard is open to the public, although anyone over sixteen must carry photo identification. A handicapped placard will allow driving onto the Yard after a vehicle security inspection. Photos of buildings and monuments may be taken. A courtesy shuttle runs from the Yard to the Navy–Marine Corps Memorial Stadium, where there is parking for a fee. Jogging is allowed in the Yard, but bicycling, rollerblading, rollerskating, and skateboarding are not.

Along the Chesapeake Bay, the walkway outside the Armel-Leftwich Visitor Center. *Courtesy Jamie Howren Photography*

who have left and then gone on to fight many wars, also far from home. Here is where that preparation begins.

ON THE BANKS OF THE SEVERN

The U.S. Naval Academy in Annapolis was established in 1845. Prior to that date, the training of naval officers had taken place haphazardly aboard ships at sea. Subsequently, small naval schools were set up in multiple locations around the country, but the training was neither comprehensive nor consistent. The prevailing sentiment in the mid-nineteenth century kept the training focus at sea: "You could no more educate sailors in a shore college, than you could teach ducks to swim in a garret."[1] Over time, and with the advent of steam, Navy ships became more technologically advanced, and opponents to a naval college began to acquiesce. But it wasn't until George Bancroft, a man who valued history and education, was appointed Secretary of the Navy by the new president,

James K. Polk, that a successful effort was made to acquire a location and establish a curriculum for a formal Naval Academy under the auspices and supervision of the government.

The old and obsolete Fort Severn at Annapolis was deemed an ideal location for both academic, nautical, and gunnery training. The fort was situated on a piece of land at the juncture of the Severn River and the Chesapeake Bay. Erected in 1808, it was surrounded by a nine-foot-high brick wall that ran along the water. Inside was a circular battery, armed with ten heavy guns and topped with a conical-shaped sod roof.[2] Historical accounts cite the fort as critical to the city's defense during the War of 1812.[3] Bancroft thought it was an ideal location for the Naval Academy, and so the land was transferred from the War Department on 15 August 1845. Since Fort Severn was already owned by the government, Bancroft did not have to approach Congress for permission to take possession, thus avoiding any opposition.

PART I *The quadrangle*

The quadrangle

A *Walk in the Yard* has been divided into two self-guided walking tours: an "inner" tour and an "outer" or "perimeter" tour. The inner tour covers the Quadrangle and the main buildings of the Yard, beginning at the Armel-Leftwich Visitor Center and proceeding to the structures designed by Ernest Flagg at the turn of the twentieth century, major buildings, monuments, and sites. The "outer" tour of the perimeter of the Yard—also beginning at the Visitor Center—takes visitors along the Sea Wall, explores the monuments and sites tucked along the edge of the Yard, investigates the contemporary structures designed by John Carl Warnecke in the 1960s and 1970s, and looks closely at the Cemetery and Columbarium. For those visitors with more time and energy—and better walking shoes—this extended tour is worth the time.

The Armel-Leftwich Visitor Center, considered the "front door" to approximately 1.5 million visitors each year. *Courtesy CSD Architects*

THE ARMEL-LEFTWICH VISITOR CENTER

The Armel-Leftwich Visitor Center is a short walk from downtown Annapolis, just inside Gate One (at the corner of King George and Randall streets in downtown Annapolis), and the ideal place to get an overview of the Yard, a general background of and orientation to the Naval Academy, and a personally guided walking tour by an official Naval Academy tour guide.

Two plaques greet visitors en route to the Visitor Center: the larger plaque recites the Naval Academy's mission and the smaller one, placed in 1963 by the Department of the Interior, officially designates the Yard a national historic landmark.

The Visitor Center is situated at the edge of the Sea Wall, overlooking the Annapolis Harbor (Spa Creek). With healthy winds and good weather for almost eight months out of the year, the Sea Wall area attracts world-class professional and amateur sailors alike. With immediate access to a saltwater bay, it also provides an ideal location for training future naval leaders.

Designed by CSD Architects of Baltimore, the Center serves as a symbolic "front door" to the Yard, from the waterfront and downtown Annapolis, to approximately 1.5 million visitors each year. Named for Capt. Lyle Oliver Armel II and Lt. Col. William Groom Leftwich Jr., both alumni of the Class of 1953, the Center opened in 1995 as part of the Academy's 150th anniversary. Plaques just inside the entrance to this building pay tribute to the lives and careers of these two men.

The Visitor Center is open 9 AM–5 PM from March to December and 9 AM–4 PM in January and February. Guided walking tours of the Yard start here and last one hour and fifteen minutes. There are public restrooms, snack machines, a large gift shop, and tables and benches inside and out for visitors to rest. Questions on guided

The lobby of the Visitor Center. *Courtesy CSD Architects*

walking-tour times and fees can be directed to the Visitor Center's main phone number (410-263-6933) or by checking its website at www.navyonline.com. All proceeds from the tour fee and the sale of merchandise support Brigade of Midshipmen activities.

The entire Visitor Center building was designed with a naval and sailing flavor, from the massive mast in the gift shop that extends two floors to inlaid boat and semaphore flag patterns on the floor. On its first floor, the Center displays numerous colorful maps and pictorial highlights of the Academy and the Yard, with touch screens that can call up specific buildings and areas of interest. A theater offers a short film that portrays the life of a midshipman. The film shows midshipmen in class, engaged in sports activities, and aboard ship on their summer training cruises. It gives laymen a glimpse at what training for the military life entails.

The Graduates in Space exhibit is on display on the first floor. It chronicles the story of Rear Adm. Alan

Shepard, alumnus of the Class of 1945, who flew the *Freedom 7* capsule for fifteen minutes during a suborbital flight on 5 May 1961, signaling the beginning of the Space Age in the United States. To date, a total of fifty-three Naval Academy graduates have been accepted into our nation's space program; a short video in this exhibit highlights their careers.

A model of the USS *Maryland* (BB-46), built by Arthur Eresman of Kettering, Ohio, a former crewmember of the original battleship, is also on display on the first floor. The USS *Maryland* survived the Japanese attack on Pearl Harbor and was used as a warship until the end of World War II. The USS *Maryland*'s set of presentation silver is on display at the Maryland State House in downtown Annapolis.

The staircase to the second floor of the Visitor Center.
Courtesy CSD Architects

Visitors can examine a Dahlgren boat howitzer, designed by Rear Adm. John A. Dahlgren and used both aboard ship and on land during the American Civil War. More guns and cannons can be found in the park area in front of Dahlgren Hall.

Finally, the gift shop offers a wide selection of Naval Academy, U.S. Navy, and nautical mementos for purchase.

A large staircase leads to the second floor of the Visitor Center. Among numerous interactive exhibits there is a sample midshipman's room. Also on the second

A Visitor Center display, depicting a midshipman engaged in physical training. *Courtesy CSD Architects*

floor is an exhibit dedicated to the career of Capt. John Paul Jones, whose crypt can be found under the Chapel. The original wooden figurehead of the USS *Delaware*, Tamanend (commonly called "Tecumseh"), and a Medal of Honor exhibit that details the seventy-three U.S. Naval Academy graduates who have received our nation's highest award for valor are also part of the second-floor display. A bronze replica of Tecumseh stands in front of Bancroft Hall.

The rest of this area is dedicated to midshipman life, with a sample midshipman room so visitors can see exactly how students live. The balconies of the second floor offer a stunning view of the Yard and Annapolis Harbor. Stationary binoculars are available; on a clear day, viewers can spy the twin spans of the Chesapeake Bay Bridge.

The Center's architects intentionally created a vast bay window for visitors to enjoy, as well as to entice those who can see the Center from the water.[4]

The Zimmerman Bandstand. *Courtesy Jamie Howren Photography*

To begin the self-guided walking tour, step outside the front door. Areas that are accessible to the physically disabled are marked. Head down King George Street, take the first right onto Cooper Road, and then the first left onto Porter Road, passing officer housing and Ward Hall. Take the first right up Buchanan Road. Walk past Buchanan House (the house with the circular driveway) and look to the left to find the Zimmerman Bandstand. Our walk in the Quadrangle officially begins here. While not the actual center of the Yard, the Bandstand is an ideal place for a 360-degree view of this storied place called the Yard.

Charles A. Zimmerman. *Courtesy Special Collections & Archives Division, Nimitz Library, U.S. Naval Academy*

The U.S. Naval Academy Band, assembled in the original "gazebo," 1897. *Courtesy Special Collections & Archives Division, Nimitz Library, U.S. Naval Academy*

THE ZIMMERMAN BANDSTAND

The Zimmerman Bandstand, built in 1922, is surrounded by boxwoods, azaleas, and oak trees, giving visitors a pastoral and somewhat elevated view of the heart of the Yard, or the "Quadrangle," while they enjoy the sounds of the Chapel bell and the clock tower at Mahan Hall. Its namesake, Charles A. Zimmerman, was the Academy's official bandmaster at the turn of the twentieth century and was the composer of "Anchors Aweigh," the Navy's official song. First sung on 1 December 1906, "Anchors Aweigh" was accompanied by lyrics written by Midn. Alfred Hart Miles. Composing a march for each graduating class was a tradition upheld every year by Bandmaster Zimmerman. Most of the marches were soon forgotten, but this football fight song had staying power.

If you stand on the bandstand and slowly rotate your gaze in a full circle, notice the buildings that surround you. The architect of this collection of Beaux-Arts buildings, Ernest Flagg, designed the Quadrangle in the form of a cross, with each point symbolically representing a specific element of a midshipman's Academy training. There is:

- The Chapel in front of you, representing the moral, or spiritual, element of development;
- The complex of Sampson, Maury, and Maha halls, ninety degrees from the Chapel, representing the academic center for the Brigade of Midshipmen;

HISTORIC MARKERS

Behind the Zimmerman Bandstand, along Soley Walk (toward Bancroft Hall), is a small plaque marking the former location of Nicholson House, briefly used as the official residence of the Commandant of Midshipmen and formerly owned by Judge Joseph H. Nicholson, the man who suggested to Francis Scott Key that a poem he wrote be turned into "The Star-Spangled Banner."[5] Judge Nicholson's wife was the sister of Mrs. Key.

THE FREEDOM TREE
Behind the bandstand, on the other side of Davidson
Walk, is the Freedom Tree, a tulip poplar that was dedi-
cated in 1973 to all U.S. Naval Academy POWs and
MIAs (those Navy personnel who were held as prisoners
of war or who were reported as missing in action).

- The Annapolis Harbor, which can be seen between the more contemporary Michelson and Chauvenet halls, representing the place where the midshipmen develop their nautical, or professional, skills;
- Bancroft Hall, where the midshipmen live and socialize, an integral part of the midshipmen's lives during their four years at the Academy.

Depending on the time of day or day of week, you can hear students laughing while walking to class, the Chapel bells chiming, the brigade marching to a parade at Worden Field, or a small group of midshipmen jogging by on an early morning run. You might even hear the crew team rowing nearby on the Severn River. The Yard is always alive with sounds, the sounds of Academy routines.

The Herndon Monument, adjacent to the Zimmerman Bandstand, was erected in 1860 in an area in the Yard that, at the time, was surrounded by faculty quarters.
Courtesy Jamie Howren Photography

Midshipmen relaxing around the Herndon Monument, 1873.
Courtesy Special Collections & Archives Division, Nimitz Library, U.S. Naval Academy

THE HERNDON MONUMENT

As you step down from the Zimmerman Bandstand, take a closer look at the Herndon Monument. This massive shaft of Quincy granite was placed in its current spot in 1860 as a memorial to Cdr. William Lewis Herndon, who died in 1857 when his mail steamer *Central America* sank in a storm off the coast of Savannah, Georgia. Commander Herndon made gallant efforts to save his ship. A rescue boat stood nearby and managed to save many of the passengers. When Commander Herndon realized his death was imminent, he donned his dress uniform to go down with the ship and the rescue boats witnessed his stark figure salute and disappear—in full dress uniform. A committee of Navy and Marine Corps officers was formed only thirteen days later to raise $1,161 to commission the monument.

In 1907, the Herndon Monument took on new significance for plebes (U.S. Naval Academy freshmen) when they swarmed the monument to celebrate the new privileges they attained as Youngsters (sophomores). One of those privileges included the freedom to walk around "Lover's Lane," the area surrounding Herndon where midshipmen courted young women on Sunday afternoons. In the 1940s, this rite of passage began to include the ritual of climbing the monument, culminating with a midshipman perching himself at the pinnacle of the twenty-one-foot obelisk (ouch!). As early as 1947, the ritual began to include placing an upperclassman's "cover" (hat) at the top

"Lover's Lane," circa 1890. *Courtesy Special Collections & Archives Division, Nimitz Library, U.S. Naval Academy*

of the monument. In 1949, the climbing ritual took on new difficulties when the obelisk was greased.

Since 1962, the Academy has recorded the amount of time each class has taken to climb Herndon and replace the plebe's cover with an upperclassman's cover. The longest recorded time was the Class of 1998, which took four hours, five minutes, and seventeen seconds to dislodge the cover. The quickest recorded time was the Class of 1972,

The Class of 2008 climbing the greased Herndon Monument.
Courtesy Jamie Howren Photography

which took one minute and thirty seconds to topple
the cover. Legend also has it that the midshipman who
unseats the cover from the tip of the Herndon obelisk will
become the class's first admiral.

When you walk around the circumference of the
monument, it is hard to believe the destructive activity
that takes place every May when the class of 1,000-plus
plebes descends on the greased monument, scrambling
over each other to reach the top. The defacing—albeit
temporary and sanctioned—is unique and attracts thou-
sands of spectators every year. The monument bears little
wear and tear from its annual attack and the grass around
Herndon continues to grow—thanks to a dedicated group
of gardeners and a talented cleaning crew who hose
down the grease and add more grass the evening after the
annual ritual.

From Herndon, you can get a glimpse of most of the
buildings that make up the largest collection of American

Beaux-Arts architecture in the United States. And they were all designed by one man, Ernest Flagg.

ARCHITECT OF THE "NEW" ACADEMY

Ernest Flagg, the renowned twentieth-century architect, built the "new" Naval Academy in the early 1900s and infused a sense of grandeur into the Yard—physical structures befitting the training ground for the world's preeminent Navy.

It was, indeed, Congress' intention to replace the rundown set of buildings on the old Fort Severn grounds. Originally designed in 1896, just three years after the Columbian Exposition in Chicago, the "new" Naval Academy was designed to represent the best of French and American exposition architecture. It is now recognized as Flagg's most monumental accomplishment.[6]

When Flagg first examined the existing buildings in the Yard, they were in quite a state of disrepair. "With the exception of the governors' house and the old fort," Flagg wrote, "there are no buildings of any interest or beauty on the grounds. All are old, poorly built, and many of them are much in need of repair. Some have recently been condemned as unsafe, and several have been torn down for this reason. It seems to have been the policy of the Government to build here in the poorest way, and to place the buildings wherever there was a vacant place,

---

DESIGN MOTIFS AROUND THE YARD
Look for symbols of oak (represents strength), oak leaves (a traditional Navy symbol), and laurel (represents victory), as well as nautical symbols—anchors (also represent hope), ships, and dolphins—in the architecture and artwork around the Yard. Notice these decorative motifs scattered liberally on sconces, columns, cornices, benches, and cannons.

---

with absolutely no regard to the convenient and economical working of the institution."[7]

By contrast, Flagg's design (which was reportedly envisioned in a one-day visit to the Yard) was coordinated and thoughtful, not building by building but rather as a complex of buildings designed to reflect the academic, physical, professional, and spiritual development of its students. The new Academy set a standard for Federal building design, as it was the first time Beaux-Arts planning was used for a large-scale government complex.[8] Multiple buildings have subsequently been added to the Flagg landscape, blurring his original vision.

Fortunately, the integrity of these structures has remained intact. The Chapel is one of the most significant.

THE CHAPEL

The skyline of Annapolis is identifiable by two peaks: the state Capitol and the Academy Chapel. Strategically placed on the highest ground in the Yard, surrounded by blooming wisteria in summer, the Chapel provides the spiritual center of activity for the Brigade of Midshipmen and the Academy community. Framed by large oak trees, the Bandstand, and Herndon Monument, the Chapel was inspired by J. Hardouin Mansart's military chapel, Dôme des Invalides,[9] and remains the focal point of the U.S. Naval Academy. Flagg had a vision of the Chapel as a type of "Pantheon of the Navy," with catacombs of prominent naval figures. He built it as part memorial and part auditorium—to serve both secular and religious needs.

Ernest Flagg originally designed all the new buildings to be constructed of red brick with limestone trim—to complement the smaller, historic structures around Annapolis. But Congressional lobbies from Maine and New Hampshire[10] were successful in passing legislation to use granite from these two states. By the time the

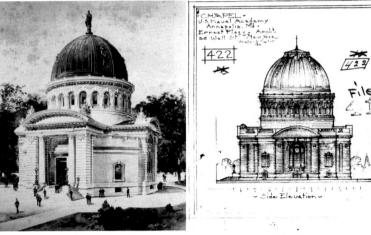

Ernest Flagg's line drawing and artist's rendition of the Chapel, circa 1898. *Courtesy Special Collections & Archives Division, Nimitz Library, U.S. Naval Academy*

The U.S. Naval Academy Chapel in summer.
Courtesy Jamie Howren Photography

DID YOU KNOW?
Placed in the Chapel cornerstone at its laying on 3 June 1904 were copies of the Naval Academy regulations, the Academy's admissions policies, the Register of the Navy, a roster of officers on duty at the Academy that year, the Annapolis newspaper Evening Capital, *and the* Baltimore Sun, *as well as autographed photos of President Roosevelt, then-Secretary of the Navy William H. Moody, then-Superintendent Capt. Williard Brownson, Ernest Flagg, and Admiral of the Navy George Dewey. Admiral Dewey laid the cornerstone that day.*

Chapel was built several years later, construction costs had increased dramatically and granite was too expensive. Flagg instead used an experimental construction process that used concrete reinforced with steel and infilled with brick. This "ferro–concrete" process[11] preserved the aesthetic look of pure granite but reduced the costs significantly.

It was considered quite radical, but the success of this process was critically lauded in architectural and scientific

The Chapel under construction, circa 1904, with faculty residences to the right. *Courtesy Special Collections & Archives Division, Nimitz Library, U.S. Naval Academy*

The bronze Chapel doors on the day they were dedicated, 1909.
Courtesy Special Collections & Archives Division, Nimitz Library, U.S. Naval Academy

journals at the time. To accommodate an increased Brigade of Midshipmen, renowned architect Paul Philippe Cret was hired in 1940 to design the expansion of the Chapel, or what was known as the "New Nave." (Cret also designed the Federal Reserve Building and the Folger Shakespeare Library in Washington, D.C.) The addition altered the original footprint of the building from that of a Greek cross with equal transepts to a Latin cross.

The Chapel's 210-foot-high dome, crafted from copper sheathing in 1929, and the gold spire can be seen from nearly anywhere within the Yard. The massive anchors on either side of the entrance, weighing 10,500 pounds each, are the traditional symbols of hope and faith and were originally cast for the Navy's armored cruiser *New York*. The towering bronze doors with vertical panels in bas-relief depict education, or "father science," and "mother patriotism" in allegorical symbols. Dedicated at an elaborate ceremony in 1909, these doors were designed by Evelyn Beatrice Longman, a young woman who was the winner of a design competition sponsored by the National

The bronze Chapel doors, showing details of Naval Academy symbols.
Courtesy Special Collections & Archives Division, Nimitz Library, U.S. Naval Academy

Sculpture Society. Gorham Manufacturing Company cast the twenty-two-foot-tall doors, which were a gift from Col. Robert Means Thompson on behalf of the Class of 1868. If you look closely, you will notice the symbols of *Invention*, a young seaman holding a torpedo, and *Science,* an aging instructor. The Naval Academy's curriculum has always been firmly rooted in the technical subjects of science and engineering. The figure of the mother teaching her son and sending him off with his fellow new recruits is a symbol that reflects the ideals of religion and patriotism. These are intended to remind midshipmen of the commitment they have made by attending the Naval Academy.

As you walk under the choir loft into the main sanctuary, the full effect of the Chapel's design is immediate. Light rays shoot in all directions, diffused by the towering stained-glass windows, including the window

---

DID YOU KNOW?
There are 6,700 pipes in the Chapel's organ. With more than 796 different controls, it can represent the sounds of 15,688 pipes.

above the altar that depicts Christ walking upon iridescent waters. Made in Tiffany studios, the Porter window is the design of Frederick Wilson, who also designed the Mason, Sampson, and Farragut windows. Officially called "Christ the Consoler," this window was presented by the Class of 1869 as a memorial to Adm. David Dixon Porter, who served as superintendent during the class' four years at the Academy. A marble piece of stone, called an "ashlar," sits above the Porter window (as it is more commonly called), inscribed with the first few words of the Navy hymn "Eternal Father Strong to Save." Composed by Reverend William Whiting upon surviving a violent storm at sea in the Mediterranean, this hymn is sung at the conclusion of most services held in the Chapel.

If you have time, all the stained-glass windows that adorn the Chapel are worth a close look for their historical and symbolic significance:

- The Farragut window, made by the Gorham Company, sits mounted on the right transept. Adm. David Glasgow Farragut, naval hero of the Civil War, is shown being guided by the Archangel Michael through the minefields of Mobile Bay.
- Sited on the left of the transept is the Sampson window, a gift from a group of servicemen of the active duty Navy in 1909. It memorializes Rear Adm. William T. Sampson, who led the Navy in victory over the Spanish fleet in the Battle of Santiago, Cuba, in 1898.
- Between the transepts sits the "Commission Invisible," another Tiffany window presented by the Class of 1927; it depicts a newly minted naval officer reading his officer's commission in the shadow of the flag and in front of the specter of Christ offering His benediction. The model for this window was Thomas J.

Front view of the Chapel, its copper dome and gold spire visible from nearly everywhere in the Yard. *Courtesy Jamie Howren Photography*

Hamilton, class president and hero of the 1926 football season.

- The Sir Galahad window, also made in the Tiffany studio, was commissioned in memory of Lt. Cdr. Theodorus Bailey Myers Mason. Sited to the left of the center aisle, it depicts a Christian knight in armor standing ready as a guardian of his country's honor.

CHAPEL WEDDING POLICY
Use of the Chapel for weddings is limited to U.S. Naval Academy alumni, military staff and faculty members, active duty military members assigned to Naval Support Activity Annapolis, and active duty personnel living in the immediate vicinity of the Chapel who also regularly attend Chapel services.[12]

DID YOU KNOW?
Rumor has it that John Phillips of the Mamas and the Papas attended the Naval Academy and wrote his famed ballad "California Dreamin'" about his experience here. In an interview on National Public Radio,[13] Phillips put that rumor to rest and explained that the song is about St. Patrick's Cathedral in New York City. Academy attendance records show, however, that a John Edmund A. Phillips did attend the Naval Academy about the time the musician would have gone to college, based on his age at the time. He would have been a member of the Class of 1958.

- The smaller windows that line the left and right aisles in the lower nave depict various biblical scenes. From the congregation's perspective, the right side depicts Old Testament scenes and the left side depicts New Testament scenes.

St. Andrew's Chapel, located underneath the main Academy Chapel. *Courtesy Special Collections & Archives Division, Nimitz Library, U.S. Naval Academy*

DID YOU KNOW?
The model ship hanging in the rear of the Chapel is a
fifteenth-century Flemish "carrack," twelve feet long,
which is hung in the tradition of votive ships found in
churches and cathedrals in Europe as a symbol to visitors
that seamen frequented the church. It was a gift of the
Navy's Construction Corps in 1941 and serves as an
unseen deity, watching over seafarers.

While midshipmen are no longer required to attend services, the Chapel still serves as an informal refuge and place for quiet reflection. Midshipmen are forbidden from being married while attending the Academy, although many choose the Chapel to tie the knot after graduating. Vice Adm. Al Burkhalter, Class of 1951, and his wife Becky were married there in 1972. It was a second marriage for both of them, with their children in attendance. The submarine USS *Jallao* was making a port visit to the Yard that day and the officers of the boat were friends with then–Captain Burkhalter. So members of the crew walked over to provide the sword arch for their friend and his new bride.

ST. ANDREW'S CHAPEL ◓
St. Andrew's Chapel, of Romanesque design, is located
underneath the nave of the main Academy Chapel.
Designed as a sanctuary for small funerals, weddings,
and baptisms, it was completed in 1940 and renovated
in 1986. St. Andrew's is replete with nautical treasures,
including a baptismal font whose pedestal and stand
are made from oaken beam timbers and a top sheet-bitt
from the USS Constitution *("Old Ironsides"). The windows*
depict lives of saints and contain symbols associated
with water.

It was a natural decision for Admiral and Mrs. Burkhalter to marry in the Yard and at the Chapel, as "the Navy was and is such a big part of our lives," says Becky (whose first husband was lost at sea on USS *Scorpion*, along with the entire submarine and crew). The imposing size of the Chapel did not make it any less intimate for them. "There's something about it that makes you feel you belong there," she says. "It's a family affair. But . . . I do remember feeling that I had to walk down a *very* long aisle."

JOHN PAUL JONES CRYPT

If you head back outside and walk around to your left, you will pass St. Andrew's Chapel and come to a set of granite steps that leads to the crypt of Revolutionary War hero John Paul Jones, most famous for his actions in a fierce battle with the British in 1779. While command- ing the USS *Bonhomme Richard* (named for Benjamin

Crypt of John Paul Jones. *Courtesy Special Collections & Archives Division, Nimitz Library, U.S. Naval Academy*

Franklin), Jones was asked by his British foe if he wanted to surrender. With broken masts and a ship full of holes from cannon and grenade attacks, Jones responded, "I have not yet begun to fight." The tone set by this darkened and subdued hallowed space is intended to evoke the image of a burial at sea.

John Paul Jones. *Courtesy Special Collections & Archives Division, Nimitz Library, U.S. Naval Academy*

This circular room, ninety-five feet in diameter, was specifically designed by Flagg as a crypt for Jones' remains, but when it was built, it was unclear as to where Jones was actually buried. Despite his victories at sea during the Revolutionary War and his heroic reputation, Jones was buried without fanfare in a nondescript cemetery in

---

JEAN-ANTOINE HOUDON

The French sculptor of the John Paul Jones bust on display in the crypt is generally considered one of the best European sculptors of the eighteenth and nineteenth centuries. Jean-Antoine Houdon's works are particularly renowned for their keen and accurate likeness to their subjects. Houdon took meticulously detailed measurements. The eyes of his subjects are strikingly penetrating. It is no surprise that this marble bust of Jones was used as a comparative link to the one-hundred-year-old corpse unearthed in France. The bust is signed by Houdon——see the inscription "J.A.H. 1781"——and was a bequest to the U.S. Naval Academy Museum by Marshall Field of Chicago in 1961. The Museum holds a total of seven copies of this bust.

Paris. In 1913, a century after his death, the United States initiated a campaign to recognize his as yet unheralded contributions to our nation's fight for independence and our country's naval traditions. The hunt was on to find his body and bring it to the Yard.

Gen. Horace Porter, Ambassador to France in 1899, was assigned the task. He conducted extensive research on death certificates and discovered a letter in the French National Archives of 1792 citing a cemetery and location, indicating that friends of Jones had arranged for his burial. Armed with old maps, cemetery records, and registration documents, Ambassador Porter located the Saint Louis Cemetery in Paris, which had been abandoned a century prior and built over with retail shops. He had Jones' body disinterred and found the corpse was remarkably well preserved in a lead casket filled with alcohol and straw. Without DNA to prove the body was indeed Jones', forensic experts at the time visually compared the skull to a bust of Jones, created by renowned sculptor Jean-Antoine Houdon in 1780 (which is on display here in the crypt). But an autopsy proved to be the definitive link, as the exhumed body had died of the same causes as Jones.

With Jones' body recovered, the nation and the U.S. Naval Academy could proceed with its grand plans to honor him, one century after his death. A ceremonial return trip and commemoration services were held in the Yard on 24 April 1906. In January 1913, John Paul Jones was finally interred in this sarcophagus, a twenty-one-ton black-and-white Royal Pyrenees marble structure designed by Whitney Warren and sculpted by Sylvain Salières. Jones is buried amid oceanic symbols, as the colors of the marble seem reminiscent of a stormy, frothy sea and the bronze dolphins that serve as physical support frolic below the coffin. The carved seaweed garlands drape the coffin like jewelry.

Surrounding the coffin in the sunken marble base of the crypt are eight black-and-white columns, which form an octagon. The gilded bronze inscriptions name the ships Jones commanded and pay tribute to the contributions he made to the early success of our nation's Navy:

John Paul Jones, 1747–1792;
U.S. Navy, 1775–1783.
He gave our Navy its earliest traditions
of heroism and victory.
Erected by Congress, A.D. 1912.

Also in the crypt:

- An original marble Houdon bust;
- Two of Jones' swords, including the one prsented to him by Louis XVI;
- The certificate, signed by George Washington, inducting Jones into the Society of the Cincinnati, the oldest veterans' organization in the United States;
- Models of two of his commands, the sloop *Providence* and the USS *Bonhomme Richard;*
- Jones' captain's commission signed by John Hancock.

BUCHANAN HOUSE AND
THE ADMINISTRATION BUILDING ●

As you leave the Chapel, cross the street again. As you look back at its monumental size, you will notice two complementary structures flanking the Chapel: the superintendent's residence, or Buchanan House, to the left and the Administration Building to the right. Farther down to the right on the other side of Maryland Avenue is the Officers' and Faculty Club and Leahy Hall (behind Preble Hall). Head toward Buchanan House, to the left of the Chapel.

The Chapel and Buchanan House. *Courtesy U.S. Naval Academy Photographic Services*

Buchanan House is the official residence of the superintendent, the Naval Academy's equivalent of a university president. Cdr. Franklin Buchanan, the home's namesake, was the first superintendent of the U.S. Naval School, as it was originally called 1845–47.

Much like the White House, Buchanan House has space for both private living and public entertaining. The superintendent's family enjoys a picturesque view of the Chapel's patinized copper dome when climbing the stairs to their private quarters. They also have a private kitchen

WHAT IS A SUPERINTENDENT?
The Naval Academy's superintendent is an active duty flag or general officer (Navy or Marine Corps) who serves in the same role at the Academy as a college president would at a civilian college.

BUCHANAN HOUSE FACTS
- *Designed by architect Ernest Flagg;*
- *Built in 1906 at a cost of $77,539;*
- *The third Yard structure built to house the Academy superintendent and his family;*
- *Named in 1976 for the Naval Academy's first superintendent*

View of Buchanan House from the back, overlooking an elaborate garden brimming with boxwood, azaleas, tulips, and many other exotic botanicals. The superintendent entertains many official guests here. *Courtesy U.S. Naval Academy Photographic Services*

and family room adjacent to, but separate from, the official entertaining spaces on the second floor. The living room is adorned with Oriental rugs, a crystal chandelier, oil paintings, and decorative moldings. Through the doorway on the far right is a portrait of First Lady Dolly Madison, hanging in the drawing room. The superintendent is responsible for entertaining numerous U.S. and foreign government officials who are visiting the Naval Academy on official business. In fact, Buchanan House

Buchanan House interior stairs, a good vantage point to view
the Chapel dome. *Courtesy Jamie Howren Photography*

Second-floor foyer from the stairway leading to the third floor of
Buchanan House. *Courtesy Jamie Howren Photography*

Buchanan House living room, one of the more formal areas the superintendent uses to entertain guests. *Courtesy Jamie Howren Photography*

DID YOU KNOW?

Many Navy ships have their own set of presentation silver, custom designed and donated by families or cities to honor a namesake ship or naval hero. Buchanan House residents entertain a large number of guests, so their collections of china and silver are used frequently. In the house collection is a set of 112 pieces of Whiting and Tiffany sterling silver platters, bowls, and even a candelabra that was originally made and donated to the armored cruiser USS New York (ACR-2) by the citizens of New York.

Navy presentation silver on display in Buchanan House. *Courtesy Jamie Howren Photography*

Table and chair at which Captain Reid sat to draft the flag resolution of 1818.
Courtesy Jamie Howren Photography

has entertained more guests than any other official government residence—second only to the White House.

Filled with antiques and fine art, Buchanan House is both a residence and a museum. The rich oil paintings that adorn the walls bear portraits of famous naval heroes, including Decatur, Perry, Farragut, Luce, Reid, Biddle, and, of course, Buchanan. Rest on a chair or lean against a table and you're touching history. Sitting in a corner in the drawing room is the desk where Capt. Samuel Chester Reid drafted the flag resolution of 1818, setting the number of stripes for the U.S. flag at thirteen—

Federal-style mirrors in the dining room were donated by the descendents of Capt. James Lawrence.
Courtesy Jamie Howren Photography

one for each original state—and proposing a star be added for each subsequent state admitted into the Union.

The dining room furniture was made specifically for this room by a Baltimore cabinetmaker, with a table that can comfortably seat twenty-four

guests. A
Waterford
chandelier was
a gift of Brig.
Gen. Luke
W. Finlay,
who is a direct
descendant of
Adm. Raphael
Semmes, a
notorious
Confederate
naval officer.
Asher Durand,

This Asher Durand painting of George Washington (1835) hangs in the Buchanan House dining room. *Courtesy Jamie Howren Photography*

a well-known painter of the Hudson River School,
produced the George Washington portrait that graces a
nearby wall. He modeled it after the famous Gilbert Stuart
work housed at the Boston Athanaeum.

To the left side of the house is the carriage entrance,
with a circular driveway and overhang to protect arriving
and departing guests from the elements. Many years ago,
strolling staff and faculty could stop by and leave their calling cards in a bowl at the carriage entrance foyer. Today,
visitors can enjoy the beauty of the house from the outside
and can even catch
a peek at the expan-
sive gardens in
the back.

Calling-card table,
located in the
"carriage entrance"
to Buchanan House.
*Courtesy Jamie Howren
Photography*

DID YOU KNOW?
Buchanan House has a bathroom named after President
Franklin D. Roosevelt, the only bathroom that we know of
named after a leader of the free world. President
Roosevelt was a frequent visitor to the superintendent's
house, as Navy ships were his preferred means of
oceanic transportation and he routinely embarked from
the seawall. The superintendent at the time installed a
first-floor "head" just for him.

For most superintendents and their families, sleeping every night in a house with such a rich heritage is considered an honor and a privilege. Living in a museum environment and being entrusted with the care of its priceless contents carry a certain responsibility for its residents. Posted on a plaque on the lower level is this reminder from President Franklin Delano Roosevelt: "I never forget . . . I live in a house owned by all the American people, and that I have been given their trust."

To the right of the Chapel is the Administration Building, housing the Naval Academy's superintendent's

The Franklin D. Roosevelt bathroom. *Courtesy Jamie Howren Photography*

offices and several other Academy officials' offices. On either side of the walkway leading to the entrance of the Administration Building are two large cannon-balls and two guns.

Cdr. Franklin Buchanan. *Courtesy Special Collections & Archives Division, Nimitz Library, U.S. Naval Academy*

The two cannon-balls are six-hundred-pound stone shot, the type used by the Turks during the conquest of Constantinople in 1453. It was typical for naval officers stationed in the Mediterranean early in the Navy's history to bring back shot they found and use it as artistic décor on naval bases. These cannonballs were brought to the Yard by Commo. John Rodgers from his visit to Constantiople in 1825 to negotiate the first treaty

---

GUARDING BUCHANAN HOUSE
Covered in ivy and perched on top of a retaining wall to the left of Buchanan House sits an imposing five-inch armored Spanish gun, captured during the Battle of Santiago, Cuba, in 1898 from the Spanish armored cruiser Maria Teresa, *the flagship of Admiral Cervera.*

---

between the United States and the Ottoman Empire. They first graced the entrance to the Naval Academy Cemetery but were later moved. The cannon to the right is a twelve-pounder, cast in 1686, and the one to the left is an eighteen-pounder, cast in 1789 and captured by the Navy from the Mexicans in California in 1847.

GATE THREE AND PREBLE HALL

On the far right of the Administration Building is Maryland Avenue and Gate Three. If you walk close to Gate Three, you'll notice two one-story structures on either side of the gates. These small gatehouses were built in 1876 and are the oldest buildings in the Yard. This gate was originally the main entrance to the Yard.

Many midshipmen have stories of sneaking out of and back into the Yard through these gates (and probably over the walls!). Successfully attempting this maneuver was traditionally called "frenching out." Class of 1921 graduate Capt. David Byerly risked expulsion when he frenched out one week before graduation. "I went to Baltimore for the night. I can't remember why—young and foolish, I guess. I risked everything for that one night out," he admits. When he returned in the wee hours of the morning, the guard at the desk, Byerly sheepishly admits, "thought I was an officer because I was out of uniform. I just walked right in."

The gatehouses at Gate Three on Maryland Avenue, 1845–67.
Courtesy Special Collections & Archives Division, Nimitz Library, U.S. Naval Academy

AUGUSTA CANNON
At the corner of Maryland Avenue and Decatur Road,
just opposite Preble Hall, sits a 4-pounder iron cannon
that rests on an iron and wooden base. It was originally
mounted on the 3rd rate, sixty-four-gun HMS Augusta,
which was sunk in the Delaware River in October 1777.
Look more closely and you will notice the mark of a
crown and the letters "G.R.," which stands for "George
Rex," or King George.

Gate Three's intricate wrought–iron grillwork and
the Indiana limestone piers that flank the entrance were
designed by Allied Architects of Washington, D.C. (There
are public restrooms available in the gatehouse.)

Turn back toward the Yard and head along Maryland
Avenue. As you cross Blake Road, you'll see Preble Hall
on your left.

Named for Commo. Edward Preble, commander
of the American fleet during the Tripolitan War, Preble
Hall was constructed in 1939 and houses the official U.S.

Preble Hall, home of U.S. Naval Academy Museum and the Rogers
model-ship collection. *Courtesy U.S. Naval Academy Museum*

The ribbon-cutting ceremony for Preble Hall in 1939.
Courtesy U.S. Naval Academy Museum

Naval Academy Museum, which contains a variety of historical Navy and Naval Academy artifacts, documents, and artwork. Particular curatorial emphasis has been given to objects that describe the role of the naval officer, the theme of leadership, and, specifically, the achievements of USNA alumni. As of 2007, Preble Hall was undergoing extensive interior renovations, significantly rearranging the museum's layout and displays.

As you walk up the front steps of the Hall, notice the wrought-iron grille doors with an ornate design. Many of the Flagg-designed buildings have similar entrances.

Naval history comes alive in Preble Hall. The museum is filled with relics, including:

- The Surrender Table. Directly from the USS *Missouri,* this table was used as the platform on which the Japanese became the vanquished power in the Pacific campaign of World War II. The document on display

Housed in Preble Hall are the Surrender Table from the USS *Missouri,* including the table and tablecloth, the chair from the HMS *Duke of York,* and the pen and uniform of Fleet Adm. Chester Nimitz (in this photo, signing the surrender). *Courtesy U.S. Naval Academy Museum*

outlines the terms of the agreement and contains the signatures of the twelve delegates who attended the surrender ceremony.

• The Worden Sword. Civil War hero Rear Adm. John Worden was presented this exquisitely designed sword by his home state of New York. Worden's family donated this sword to the Yard's collection in 1912. It was put on exhibit in Memorial Hall until it mysteriously disappeared in 1931. Seventy-three years

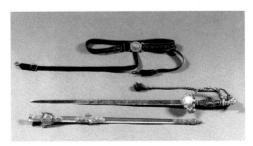

The Worden Sword. *Courtesy U.S. Naval Academy Museum*

later, in 2004, the FBI discovered the sword while investigating a group of appraisers on the TV show *Antiques Roadshow* and returned it to the Yard. Made for Tiffany, the sword's hilt depicts two scenes from the battle of the USS *Monitor* and CSS *Virginia*. The scabbard and the belt buckle are both gold-plated.

- The Rogers Collection. One of the best collections of ship models from the seventeenth, eighteenth, and nineteenth centuries, the Rogers Collection of ship models gives us an intimate record of the design of ships during the Age of Sail. Acquired by wealthy industrialist Col. Henry Huddleston Rogers beginning in 1917, this is the largest and most valuable collection of dockyard model ships in the world. They help us trace the evolution of ship design and serve as a unique source of knowledge about the great Age of Sail. In a darkened corridor of the ship model gallery is a collection of bone ship models built by French prisoners of war during the Napoleonic Wars. Spotlighted in a blue haze, the bone ship models' darkened display adds to their mystique. Many of these men were not professional sailors, but rather craftsmen who were drafted to fight in the French Navy. Their artistry and creativity are evident in the intricate and delicate use of bone scraps culled from meat rations and human or horse hair to design ship models—most likely from memory. This is the largest collection of its type in the United States.

- The Robinson Collection. While the Rogers collection demonstrates the design of ships during the Age of Sail, the Beverley R. Robinson Collection demonstrates, through a variety of media, naval engagements of the Age of Sail. Woodcuts, etchings, line engravings, mezzotints, aquatints, lithographs, and watercolors—a panoply of six thousand two-dimensional prints—

represent the work of marine artists from four centuries. Mr. Robinson's collection is distinct in its range of depictions of some of the most important naval events in world history. Some notable examples include seventy-seven Currier and Ives prints (more than half of the entire fleet of Currier and Ives naval prints)[14] and very early prints (from 1692 to 1779) that depict Spanish, French, Dutch, English, and American ships. Mr. Robinson was a distinguished New York attorney who amassed this collection over a lifetime. He was generous enough to bequeath them to the Naval Academy Museum upon his death. Several books that span the scope of the collection are available for perusal. Researchers and other interested members of the public may view the original prints and slides by making an appointment with the curator of the collection, who can be reached at (410) 293-3250.

Model ship crafted out of bone by a French POW of the Napoleonic Wars. *Courtesy U.S. Naval Academy Museum*

DOCKYARD SHIP MODELS
These unique pieces of artwork are built to scale and intricately and precisely designed. Scholars believe they were built in the same shipyards and at the same time as the real ships they represent, but it is unlikely they were used as engineering or architectural tools. As most of these models ended up in the personal collections of high-ranking officials and wealthy individuals, it is more likely that they were decorative gifts.

Dockyard ship models are recognizable by several distinctive characteristics:

- *Only the hulls are original—most of the rigging was added much later during restoration work;*
- *They are usually made of boxwood or pear wood;*
- *English dockyard models are meticulously built to a scale of 1:48;*
- *Before 1750, most of the models were framed hull construction, but left unplanked so as to view the interior. After 1750, builders began to carve the models from a single piece of wood that was hollowed out. The Robinson Collection has well-preserved examples of both types. Notable models include:* Bonhomme Richard, *the famous ship commanded by John Paul Jones that was victorious against the British ship* Serapis, *and* HMS Shannon, *the ship that defeated the* Chesapeake, *where Capt. James Lawrence famously cried, "Don't give up the ship!" as he lay dying. A flag emblazoned with this battle cry was carried into combat by Commo. Oliver Hazard Perry during the War of 1812. A replica hangs prominently in Memorial Hall.*

There are public restrooms available on the lower level of Preble Hall.

THE TRIPOLI MONUMENT

Directly behind Preble Hall, in a quiet courtyard, is one of the oldest military monuments in the United States, the Tripoli Monument. Carved from fifty-two blocks of Italian Carrera marble—mined from the same quarry used

The Tripoli Monument as seen in 1869, with Fort Severn in the background. *Courtesy Special Collections & Archives Division, Nimitz Library, U.S. Naval Academy*

by Michelangelo—this ode to heroes honors six naval officers killed in the war against Tripoli, one of the Barbary states of North Africa.

This Classical-style monument was commissioned by Capt. David Porter and other fellow officers who served in this campaign. They raised $3,000 to build it, the first naval monument to be erected anywhere in the United States. Erected in the Washington Navy Yard in 1806, the Tripoli Monument was desecrated in 1814 but restored by architect Benjamin Latrobe and relocated to the U.S. Capitol's west terrace in 1830. It was moved, once again, to the Yard in 1860.

The sculptor liberally used the human form as allegory: an angel-like figure next to the monument to symbolize "fame"; a Native American woman to symbolize our young nation; a young figure at one corner who represents "history"—or the recording of the actions of the six Tripolitan heroes who sacrificed their lives in this war; and a male figure carrying the winged staff of Mercury (now missing), which represents "commerce" and commemorates the men's role in preserving free trade. The rostral column shows ships sailing through it, a device used by the Romans to honor naval heroes. The eagle at the top carries the inscription "E pluribus unum"—"From many, one." This is the same inscription you will find on U.S. pennies.

WHAT DO YOU THINK?
Some people speculate the figures on the Tripoli monu-
ment have been shifted from their original orientation.
Look closely at how they are affixed and the direction of
the figures' gazes.

The Tripoli Monument, one of the oldest military monuments in the United States. *Courtesy Jamie Howren Photography*

Angel figure standing astride the corner of the Tripoli Monument.
Courtesy Jamie Howren Photography

HISTORIC MARKER
Across Decatur Road from Preble Hall is a ground plaque
that marks the site of the "Old Cadet Quarters," which
was one of the early dormitories that housed Academy
"cadets" (as they were called at the time). The Tripoli
Monument was situated in front of this building, which
was torn down in 1906.

LEAHY HALL AND THE ADMISSIONS OFFICE

On the other side of the Tripoli Monument is Leahy Hall,
which houses the Naval Academy Admissions Office.
Named for Fleet Adm. William Daniel Leahy, Class of
1897, who served on the Joint Chiefs of Staff and was one
of the principal architects of the Allied victory in World
War II, the hall was originally constructed in 1939 as a
medical dispensary.

Admissions Office presentations are given Monday–Friday at 9 AM, 11 AM, 2 PM, and 4 PM and on Saturdays at 9 AM and 11 AM. Information on how to apply is also available at www.usna.edu.

THE OFFICERS' AND FACULTY CLUB ●
The Tripoli Monument is connected to the Officers' and Faculty Club by a brick walkway. Also designed by Ernest Flagg, this club building was finished in 1905 and is used for entertainment and as a meeting space for professional organizations.

MAURY, MAHAN, AND SAMPSON HALLS ●
Walk back to the front of Preble Hall and head away from Gate Three along Maryland Avenue. To your left is a parking lot and courtyard that is cupped by a trio of attached buildings also designed by Ernest Flagg. These are the original academic buildings Flagg envisioned for the "new Academy." Over time, the expanding student body outgrew these classrooms, which necessitated the building of new academic buildings scattered around the Yard. Generations of midshipmen continue to spend a significant amount of academic time in these historic buildings, however. "I had a lot of classes there and I always felt connected to history when I was sitting there in those buildings," remembers John Quinn, Class of 1991. "It just felt special and I would think about the fact that I was taking classes in the same building that my dad and my granddad took classes." (John Quinn's father, Cdr. J. Thomas Quinn, is a member of the Class of 1962; his grandfather, Rear Adm. John Quinn, was a member of the Class of 1928.)

Sampson, Mahan, and Maury halls are named after three notable Academy figures. Rear Adm. William T. Sampson, the academy's thirteenth superintendent and a member of the Class of 1861, convinced Congress, in March of 1889, to reestablish specialized studies for engineers. Sampson served three tours at the U.S. Naval

Aerial view of Sampson, Mahan, and Maury halls, 1941. The field just to the right in the photo is now the Rickover Hall terrace. *Courtesy Special Collections & Archives Division, Nimitz Library, U.S. Naval Academy*

Left: Cdr. William T. Sampson. *Right:* Cdr. Alfred T. Mahan. *Courtesy Special Collections & Archives Division, Nimitz Library, U.S. Naval Academy*

Academy, more than one-third of his career. Rear Adm. Alfred T. Mahan is the U.S. Naval Academy's only midshipman ever to pass through the Academy without being a plebe. In 1877–80, he served his final tour at the Academy as head of the Ordnance Department. He wrote *The Influence of Sea Power Upon History,* the book that advocated sea power as a determinant of national strength. Cdr. Matthew Fontaine Maury was a pioneering oceanographer whose system of recording oceanographic data for ships became the worldwide standard. His 1855 book, *The Physical Geography of the Sea*, is considered the first textbook of modern oceanography. Although Flagg's original plan included granite for these three structures, delays in construction, increased labor costs, and expanding needs dictated the introduction of brick, a cheaper alternative.

The centerpiece of the trio, Mahan Hall, is classic Beaux-Arts design, with symmetry from left to right, but with diverse horizontal layers of design from bottom to top. Mahan Hall housed the Academy's library in

Mahan Hall, home of the Naval Academy library from 1907 to 1973. *Courtesy Jamie Howren Photography*

DID YOU KNOW?
The marble tablet, installed on the balustrade of Mahan Hall circa 1907, is the oldest object in the Yard that is original to the Academy. Carved in Classical style, it was originally placed on an interior wall of the old Recitation Hall, located where Tecumseh Court is now. Serving as a type of symbolic cornerstone for the Naval Academy, the tablet's inscription states, "Naval School, Founded October 10th, 1845, James K. Polk, President of the U. States, GEO. Bancroft, Secretary of the Navy."

1907–73. Note the series of coupled Palladian columns across the front and the two reclining statues on top of the central window, resting on a pediment. (We think this statue is one of only three nude women publicly displayed in the Yard.)

The original Mahan design called for statues of six admirals to be placed on the pedestals above the columns, but this plan was abandoned for budget reasons. The sconces hang to the left and right of the entrance into Mahan Hall, resembling the bow of a Roman warship—

The marble tablet, placed in the Yard soon after the Naval Academy was founded in 1845. *Courtesy Jamie Howren Photography*

The façade of Mahan Hall, adorned with intricate details of dolphins, sculptures of human beings, and leaves.
Courtesy Jamie Howren Photography

Façade decorative motif *(left)* and sconce *(right)* at Mahan Hall entrance—both with dolphin motif.
Courtesy Jamie Howren Photography

The Mahan Hall lobby. *Courtesy Jamie Howren Photography*

if viewed from their profile.[15] They have an ornate dolphin motif, a nautical theme you will find imprinted throughout the Yard—sculpted on benches, brushed in paintings, and set in stone as cornices.

Flagg consciously designed the interior common areas of Mahan Hall with vaults and platforms, intending them to hold works of art and objects of historic value.

He knew his charge was to design a training facility befitting a world-class Navy, but he also understood innately that these buildings were to be of museum-like quality and purpose, honoring the feats of naval heroes of our nation's history and reminding current students of the accomplishments of the world's greatest Navy.

The entrance vestibule of Mahan Hall is 135 feet long and 34 feet deep, with a sandstone floor. It has a central nave that is covered by a barrel vault and divided into aisles. The aisle floors are raised by steps to create platforms

The Mahan Hall grand staircase, lined with state flags and flooded with natural light, leads to the Yard's old reading room, the Hart Room. *Courtesy Jamie Howren Photography*

The ornate ceiling and lights of the Hart Room. *Courtesy Jamie Howren Photography*

to hold display objects. Opposite the front windows are six recessed glass cases that were designed to contain flags captured from British ships in the War of 1812.

Behind the vestibule is a two-flight grand staircase, lined with state flags and flooded with natural light, leading to the Hart Room, named after Adm. Thomas C. Hart, former superintendent in the 1930s. Hart was known as a progressive educator who pushed the Academy to diversify its curriculum. Resembling a plush clubroom, the Hart Room was the Academy's reading room in 1907–73. Mahan Hall served the institution as an intimate setting for academic study—but one that would not be adequate for a first-class, contemporary college's needs. The modern and cavernous Nimitz Library was completed in 1973 to accommodate the growing brigade's academic and research needs. Under glass is a scroll personally signed by all junior and senior midshipmen. It is an honor statement by which this group of midshipmen pledges not to violate the Honor Code.

Mahan Hall also has a small auditorium that is still used for small performances and lectures. It is ornately decorated, lush with historic flags, a balcony, and wooden stage, but not big enough to hold today's Brigade of Midshipmen.

An SM-2 missile on display in Maury Hall. *Courtesy Jamie Howren Photography*

DID YOU KNOW?

An inert SM-2 missile stands erect in one of the stairwells of Maury Hall. The building's 2002 renovations were completed around the missile, which extends three stories.

THE *MACEDONIAN* MONUMENT

Across Maryland Avenue from the Mahan, Maury, Sampson building trio, at the foot of Stribling Walk, is the *Macedonian* Monument. Placed here in 1925, the *Macedonian* Monument bears a figurehead of Alexander the Great, arching his neck forward. This relic of an important Navy victory pays tribute to the ship and crew of the USS *United States* that, in 1812, captured the British frigate *Macedonian*. Under the command of Capt. Stephen Decatur, the Americans decimated the British crew, killing thirty-six and wounding sixty-eight of her crew and pummeling the ship with one hundred shot in her hull and destroying her mizzenmast.[16] It was a decisive victory for the Americans that took place near the Azores.

The *Macedonian*'s flag, its figurehead, and four eighteen-pound cannons were brought to the Yard. The flag is on display in Mahan Hall and the figurehead and cannons were used as integral design elements of the monument. While many other monuments have been moved over the years, the *Macedonian* Monument is still in its original location.

The figurehead of Alexander the Great. *Courtesy Jamie Howren Photography*

The *Macedonian* Monument. Courtesy Jamie Howren Photography

THE MEXICAN WAR MONUMENT

As you proceed farther down Stribling Walk, back toward the center of the Quadrangle, you will get a clear vantage point of all the Flagg-designed buildings in the Yard. This is a frequently traversed path for midshipmen heading to and from classes in Mahan, Maury, Sampson, Chauvenet, or Michelson. Like these Academy students, you will also run right into the Mexican War Monument.

It is also called the Midshipmen's Monument because it was funded and commissioned by midshipmen to commemorate their shipmates who were killed during the Mexican–American War (1846–48). Midn. Thomas B. Shubrick, John W. Pillsbury, John R. Hynson, and Henry A. Clemson were memorialized in this Egyptian-style, marble obelisk. First erected in 1848, it has been in place at the Naval Academy longer than any other memorial in the Yard;[17] however, this is not its original location. Moved twice, the Mexican Monument landed at its present location—at the center of Stribling Walk and in the path between the Chapel and Radford Terrace (separating Michelson and Chauvenet halls)—in 1909. Notice the upright cannons supporting the marble shaft of the monument. The guns placed at each corner of the Mexican Monument were added at a later date. Originally, there were cannon balls atop the four piles of shot at the corners of the pedestal, but they disappeared—with the last one vanishing in 1986.

The Mexican War Monument, with Maury and Michelson halls in the background. *Courtesy Jamie Howren Photography*

Cannon at the Mexican Monument. *Courtesy Jamie Howren Photography*

THE SELF-ORIENTING SUNDIAL

From the Mexican Monument, you can look toward the Severn River and see a small sundial that indicates both time and direction. It was designed by Robert S. Owendoff, Class of 1968, and installed at the Academy the same year.

THE GARDENS

The grounds in the Yard are maintained by a large landscaping crew that works year-round to maintain the grass, athletic fields' turf, and garden beds. (The U.S. Naval Academy Garden Club provides holiday decorations on the entrance gates and other highly trafficked areas.) One landscape architect is responsible for the lush gardens of

DID YOU KNOW?
German POWs were used as grounds maintenance
workers in the Yard during World War II.

the Superintendent's house, as it is used extensively
for entertaining.

As new buildings are added to the Yard, trees are
inevitably cut down for construction. It is the policy of
the grounds program manager to plant three to five trees
for every one that is cut down. In 2006, more than two
hundred flowering trees were planted around the Yard,
specifically to provide more year-round natural color in
the Yard. Among those planted were cherry, crape myrtle,
silver maple, and dogwood trees.

TECUMSEH

Before you get to the clearing at the end of Stribling
Walk, you will see the back of a statue of a Native
American with a quiver of arrows strapped over his shoul-
der. If you walk around to the front of statue, you will get
a sharp view of the fierce face of this warrior.

The Tecumseh sculpture facing Bancroft Hall is a
bronze replica of a wooden figurehead that was once
attached to the USS *Delaware*, a 74-gun ship-of-the-line
that was built between 1817 and 1821. The *Delaware* was
destroyed in 1861 to prevent her from being confiscated
by the Confederates during the Civil War. However,
the figurehead was salvaged and brought to the Naval
Academy as early as 1868.

Designed to portray the great Indian chief Tamanend
of the Delaware tribe—a lover of peace and a friend of
William Penn—it captured the imagination of the midshipmen of the day, who gave it various names: Powhatan,
King Philip, and "Old Sebree" (due to the figurehead's
resemblance to Rear Adm. Uriel Sebree, Class of 1867).

The original wooden Tecumseh figurehead, in the Yard circa 1920.
*Courtesy Special Collections & Archives Division, Nimitz Library,
U.S. Naval Academy*

The bronze Tecumseh statue in the Yard, a replica of the USS
Delaware figurehead. *Courtesy Jamie Howren Photography*

Somehow, the moniker Tecumseh stuck and the figurehead took on a patron-saint role for the Brigade of
Midshipmen, who assigned him supernatural powers and
admired his proud, stern demeanor. Over time, weather
took its toll on the wooden figurehead, which was moved

indoors in 1920, and a bronze replica replaced it in the Yard.[18] The original is on display in the Visitor Center.

This fierce-looking friend is the unofficial mascot of the Brigade of Midshipmen, as well as a source of good luck in academics and sports. He is frequently decorated with paint for home football games to motivate the team and the brigade. He is a type of kindred spirit to midshipmen: "It has been surmised by competent surmisers that the wooden midshipmen found a kinship with this wooden Indian, and paid their compliments to him in their hours of need in the primitive manner of superstitious man since the first Medicine Man pranced about in his war feathers to scare away the spirits of evil."[19]

There are other ship figureheads placed around the Yard. Two notable examples are on display in the stairwell leading from Smoke Hall down to King Hall. A portrayal of *Winged Victory* holding an eagle above her head and standing on a dolphin is from the USS *Olympia*, Admiral Dewey's flagship at the Battle of Manila Bay. Opposite is a

The USS *Olympia* figurehead *(left)* and a wooden effigy of Andrew Jackson *(right)*, both on display in Smolke Hall. *Courtesy Jamie Howren Photography*

wood effigy of President Andrew Jackson, which was the figurehead on the USS *Constitution*. Bronze replicas of figureheads can also be seen in Dahlgren Hall. (A complete list of statues and busts is listed on page 179.)

FIRST- AND SECOND-CLASS BENCHES

Facing Tecumseh is a pair of benches that were originally located next to midshipmen quarters and reserved for junior and senior midshipmen. A combination of wood and copper, they are Gothic in style, complemented with platforms that have geometric stone paving. Behind each of them is a pair of cannons captured in the Mexican War with ornate and mythological creatures etched on the barrels.

CLASS OF 1897 BENCH

Behind Tecumseh is a bench called "Exedra," alluding to the ancient Greek and Roman term for an outdoor portico with seats that were used as a place for discussion.

Made of granite and limestone, this Classical structure has delicately carved dolphin and wave designs on both ends and a class crest on the back. A gift of the Class of 1897

A view of midshipmen from behind the first- and second-class benches, as Tecumseh stands guard.
Courtesy Jamie Howren Photography

on the occasion of their fortieth anniversary, the benches hold a hermetically sealed copper box encased in their foundation that contains coins, a Naval Academy yearbook (Lucky Bag 1897), and Academy Registers.[20]

Worn dolphins adorning the first- and second-class benches.
Courtesy Jamie Howren Photography

VIRGIN CANNONS

If you turn around and face Bancroft Hall, you will see a pair of cannons facing each other at the entrance to Tecumseh Court. This pair of bronze relics from the 1800s, the notorious Virgin Cannons, sits on a three-foot-high stone wall and seems to guard the entrance to Bancroft Hall. They were captured in 1847 at Vera Cruz in the Mexican War. A lion's face is sculpted on the rear of one of the Virgin Cannons. Notice the detail of the oak leaves that creates the mane and the water being blown from the lion's mouth as if he were roaring.

Legend has it that if a virgin walks by them, the cannons will detonate. They never have . . . except in 1959. In the middle of a noon formation (the weekly ritual where the Brigade of Midshipmen assembles and marches to lunch), a group of mischievous plebes set off a flawless prank.

Lion head detail on one of the Virgin Cannons. *Courtesy Jamie Howren Photography*

As described by Class of 1962 alumnus Emil D. Di Motta Jr.:

> The noon meal formation was a prelude to liberty in town with friends and relatives. The air was filled with anticipation. John, one of my classmates, and I stepped into the ranks and stood at attention. The court was filled with neat rows of midshipmen in tropical white uniforms. . . . A hand, high in a window [of Bancroft Hall], dropped. Electricity raced down the thin copper wire, vaporizing it. Down the hall, out the window and down the building, it raced. Along the wall, up the granite block, into the mouth of each cannon. Down the barrel into a plastic bag, then into the fuse of a cherry bomb tightly packed in gunpowder. And thunder roared as flame flashed from the mouths of the cannons.

Smoke bellowed into the courtyard. And then
there was absolute silence. Not a single man
flinched. The sound still reverberated from the
granite walls. Five seconds passed, then ten and
still nothing. Years of training had instilled a
respect for the unexpected.[21]

The plebes of the Class of 1962 had successfully made
their mark on the history of the Naval Academy.

Virgin Cannons frame the entrance to Tecumseh Court.
Courtesy U.S. Naval Acdemy Photographic Services

Tecumseh Court and Bancroft Hall. *Courtesy Jamie Howren Photography*

TECUMSEH COURT

During the summer, oak trees provide a verdant and soft frame to Tecumseh Court and Bancroft Hall. On both stormy and sunny days, the building casts a formidable shadow onto the courtyard that looms large. It echoes with the shouts, laughter, and struggles of generations of men (and three decades of women) learning, training, striving and testing themselves to their physical, mental and emotional limits—preparing themselves for sacrifice, for leadership, and ultimately for war.

Named for Secretary of the Navy George Bancroft, who founded the Naval Academy, it is a grand building architecturally and one of the highlights of Flagg's design. It has a deep "forecourt" with a large entrance gate. Much like Flagg's library designs and his original design for the Corcoran Gallery of Art in Washington, D.C., Bancroft

Hall exhibits as much of his personal style as it does French academic classicism and naval imagery consistent with French military architecture.[22]

Note the Naval Academy coat of arms over the main entrance (and in bronze in the bricks at the entrance to Tecumseh Court), and the ship models and granite dolphins placed on the corners of the roofline. The bronze door is six inches thick, cored hollow. Notice also that every wing has different cornice designs. The large domes (probably intended to represent globes) on each side of the

Left: The main door of Bancroft Hall, with the Naval Academy coat of arms. *Right:* Ship detail on the Bancroft Hall rooftop. *Courtesy Jamie Howren Photography*

rooftop are mirrored on the back side of the building, but the orbs are much larger there.

Directly below the pair of circular ramps that lead to the top of the main staircase (and serve as the brigade route to and from the inside of the building when in formation) are two historic bells, the Perry Bell and the *Enterprise* Bell.

View of Bancroft Hall; on the far left is the Perry Bell and to the right of the steps is the *Enterprise* bell. *Courtesy Jamie Howren Photography*

George Bancroft, as Secretary of the Navy, circa 1845. *Courtesy Special Collections & Archives Division, Nimitz Library, U.S. Naval Academy*

Left: Decorative motif adorning a corner of Bancroft Hall. *Courtesy Jamie Howren Photography. Right:* A midshipmen color guard marches in front of Bancroft Hall. *Courtesy U.S. Naval Academy Photographic Services*

THE PERRY BELL

A replica of the original Japanese bell was given to the United States in 1854 and received by Commo. Matthew Calbraith Perry upon his return from a mission to Japan to open the seaports to American commerce. The original bronze, clapper-less temple bell (on the left as you face Bancroft Hall) is more than five hundred years old and was presented to the Academy in 1858 by Commodore Perry's widow. During the early 1900s, the Perry Bell was located near the Zimmerman Bandstand. On V-J Day, midshipmen used bowling pins from the Bancroft Hall bowling alley (no longer in existence) to beat the bell as a celebration of victory. The original was returned to the people of Okinawa in 1987 and a replica was placed in its stead. The inscription translates to an admonition that barbarians will invade if Japanese leaders do not act justly.[23]

HISTORIC MARKER
In the middle of Tecumseh Court is a small brass
plaque that marks the exact spot where Cdr. Franklin
Buchanan assembled the first instructors and midshipmen
in front of the old "Recitation Hall" and formally estab-
lished the "Naval School" at Annapolis at 11AM on
10 October 1845.

The Perry Bell, a fixture in the Yard since 1858. *Courtesy Special Collections & Archives Division, Nimitz Library, U.S. Naval Academy*

THE *ENTERPRISE* BELL

Opposite the Perry Bell is another bronze bell, but one that is of a more classical style. It was taken from the World War II aircraft carrier USS *Enterprise* and mounted to the entrance of Bancroft Hall. Both the Perry Bell and the *Enterprise* Bell are rung when Navy beats Army in football.

Head up the ramps and into the rotunda of Bancroft Hall and enter the world of the Brigade of Midshipmen.

The *Enterprise* Bell, traditionally rung after Navy athletic victories. *Courtesy Jamie Howren Photography.*

BANCROFT HALL

Nothing symbolizes the heart and soul of the Yard more than the massive dormitory of Bancroft Hall. A mini-city, "Mother B" is the heart of the Naval Academy and the place midshipmen spend most of their time during their four years in Annapolis. Among the largest residential halls in the world, Bancroft Hall comprises eight wings

DID YOU KNOW?
Long-standing custom dictated that a midshipman who decided to resign from the Academy was required to stand on the "Christ, I resign," or "CIR," brick in Tecumseh Court and publicly announce his departure. According to a 1938 book called Annapolis Today,[24] *the CIR brick "may be found just thirteen paces in front of the ancient cannon at the right of the main entrance of Bancroft Hall, as you face it."*

The front entrance to Bancroft Hall. *Courtesy Jamie Howren Photography*

Archival photo of Bancroft Hall in winter, prior to the construction of Michelson and Chauvenet halls. *Courtesy Special Collections & Archives Division, Nimitz Library, U.S. Naval Academy*

spread over thirty-three acres, with 4.8 miles of corridors and more than 1,800 dorm rooms, a 55,000-square-foot department store, a barber shop, a tailor shop, a cobbler shop, a pistol range, a post office (Bancroft Hall has its own zip code!), a radio station, a credit union, and an after-hours snack shop. An adjoining dining facility, King Hall, seats 4,464.

But Bancroft Hall is more than just a dorm; it is "home" for four-thousand-plus midshipmen who come from all regions of the country, all ethnic and racial backgrounds and socioeconomic levels, living out their days in close quarters and under a strict regimen. Four years later, they emerge as young men and women, armed with a bachelor of science degree and a foundation of military training to serve in increasingly responsible leadership roles in the U.S. Navy and U.S. Marine Corps.

Bancroft Hall under construction in 1902. *Courtesy Special Collections & Archives Division, Nimitz Library, U.S. Naval Academy*

When designing Bancroft Hall, Ernest Flagg reviewed the designs and layouts of the old dormitory quarters of the Naval Academy, which by the late 1800s were in dire physical conditions: drafty, cramped, and unsafe. Flagg set about to design living quarters that were not only fitting to a naval school that was training men for a world-class Navy but that were also comfortable and featured the most modern amenities available at that time. This included luxurious "rain baths" in the bathrooms. "'I think I deserve credit for their introduction, and for this feature, at least, the thanks of the midshipmen.' Flagg believed the baths were more prized by the young men than all the other improvements combined (electric lights, automatic mail, chutes). When the architect asked a midshipman how he liked the baths, the midshipman replied, 'I have used mine seven times today.'"[25]

THE ROTUNDA

Looking up toward the Rotunda, you may feel as though you are looking into a sky of shining constellations. As

The dome of the Rotunda. *Courtesy Jamie Howren Photography*

you enter it, you will notice a grand staircase in front of you. It leads up to Memorial Hall, one of the most sacred places in the Yard. The Rotunda is also a major through-way between wings of Bancroft Hall and serves as a main reception area for guests and visitors. The patterned floor is 1.5 inches thick and incorporates inlay with four different marbles: Alps Green, light Serpentine, Longnedoc, and Old Convent Sienna.

Above the columns that line each wall are some secret rooms called the "catacombs." Until the Levy Center was opened in September 2005, these small, sequestered spaces were allegedly used by the Honor Court to administer punishment for those midshipmen accused of honor offenses (lying, cheating, stealing). There are also stories of pranksters dropping bags of flour on groups of midshipmen assembling below. Behind you, above the bronze doors is a mural painted by Dwight Sheplar, a renowned combat artist, that depicts the USS *South Dakota* in the Battle of Santa Cruz Islands in World War II in 1942. The portraits on either side of the bronze doors are of James K. Polk, president at the time of the founding of the Naval

The grand entry to Memorial Hall from the second-floor balcony of the Rotunda, circa 1938. *Courtesy Special Collections & Archives Division, Nimitz Library, U.S. Naval Academy*

The Samoan Hurricane window. *Courtesy Jamie Howren Photography*

Dolphin sconces are found throughout the Rotunda. *Courtesy Jamie Howren Photography*

Academy, by Thomas C. Cole, and George Bancroft, by
Gustave Richter.

As you head up the stairs, you will notice a large
stained-glass window mounted on the righthand side of
the hallway. Honoring casualties of an 1889 hurricane, this
piece is one of the few relics saved from one of the old
chapels in the Yard.

Public restrooms are located inside the Main Office
corridor just off the right of the Rotunda.

The limestone staircase in the Rotunda leads to Memorial Hall.
Courtesy Jamie Howren Photography

MEMORIAL HALL

As you leave the rotunda of Bancroft Hall and head up
the grand staircase in front of you toward Memorial Hall,
take a deep breath and clear your mind. The sounds of
"Mother B" will follow you throughout the passageways
of this large dormitory but will fade away as you step into
the quietude of Memorial Hall. Four chandeliers are suspended from the ceiling. Hand-cut from Czechoslovakian

lead crystal by Rambusch Studios and hung in 1964, each chandelier is approximately sixteen feet tall and contains 20,000 crytals. Fiber optics was installed in 2003 so the bulbs can be individually adjusted with a dial. The room can be lit with 124 different shades of light.

The Rambusch chandeliers in Memorial Hall. *Courtesy Jamie Howren Photography.*

As you enter the room, listen closely for the echoes of valor, of bloodshed among friends and brothers, of heroism and sacrifice. Of history. Memorial Hall is all this and more. Aside from the Chapel, it is the most sacred place in the Yard. Col. John Ripley, Class of 1962, captures the significance aptly: "This is the Sistine Chapel of the Navy. It's not the same as a chapel, but there's a deep, deep reverence of dignity, overwhelming dignity of this place that can't be replicated anywhere."

What you notice first is the imposing message on the wall directly across from the entry: "Don't give up the ship." A little more than three months after Capt. James Lawrence uttered these famous words as he lay dying aboard the frigate *Chesapeake,* providing encouragement to his crew not to surrender to the HMS *Shannon,* this flag was broken aboard the USS *Lawrence* by Oliver Hazard Perry to initiate the Battle of Lake Erie.[26] This irregularly shaped flag, with uneven letters that are so obviously hand-stitched, virtually blares at you not to forget this admonition. It is not only a reminder of a critical battle in our nation's history but also a reminder that this represents a tenet of naval service: Never surrender; maintain honor. As you walk around the perimeter of this room, you can learn of countless examples of individuals who gave their lives to uphold these ideals.

Commodore Perry's battle flag. *Courtesy U.S. Naval Academy Photographic Services*

Notice the oak leaf, eagle, dolphin, laurel, and sea-wave motifs scattered throughout the artwork and moldings. The smoothness of the limestone and stucco walls runs softly in undulating lines around the room and are graciously appointed with paintings, busts, plaques, and dioramas. The towering windows flood the room and parquet wood floors with warm light and offer glimpses of the Severn River, the Chesapeake Bay, and even the Eastern Shore. Doors lead to a balcony with a panoramic view. Rear Adm. Robert McNitt, Class of 1938, remembers, "My favorite place is the balcony.

We mustered there every month and were read to from the UCMJ [Uniform Code of Military Justice]. We didn't pay attention at the time, but I do remember the words: 'He who shall pusillanimously surrender his ship to the enemy will be punished as a court martial will direct.' Standing on that balcony, there was almost a compelling force, something drawing me in that direction—almost like a compass—telling me, 'You're going to sea.'"

As you tour the room, take a look at:

- "Ripley At The Bridge." The heroic and historic actions taken by then-Capt. John Ripley, USMC, during the 1972 Easter Offensive in South Vietnam is depicted in this low-lit diorama off to the left of the entryway (just before you enter Memorial Hall). Ripley was awarded the Navy Cross for his single-handed, successful effort to plant and detonate demolition charges under the center of a bridge, thereby blocking the movement of a large contingent of North Vietnamese regulars into the capital of the Quang Tri province. His exploits are also captured in a book called simply *The Bridge at Dong Ha* by John Girder Miller.

- "Capture of U505." Commissioned and donated by the Class of 1962, this diorama depicts the 1944 capture of the only U-boat by the U.S. Navy in World War II. The escort carrier, the USS *Guadalcanal,* commanded by Capt. Daniel V. Gallery, Class of 1921, along with five destroyers, accosted the German submarine 150 miles off the coast of French West Africa and forced it to the surface with depth charges. An American crew saved the U505 when it was abandoned by its German crew. An exhibit, which includes the U505, can be viewed at the Museum of Science and Industry in Chicago.

- The encased scroll directly below the Perry flag contains the names of all alumni killed in action against the enemy.
- The mural just above the Perry flag is a depiction of the Battle of Lake Erie in 1813 and was painted by both Charles Robert Patterson and Howard Barclay French. The murals and paintings in the room are the works of these two prolific marine artists. Patterson went to sea for the first time at age thirteen. He became a marine painter in his early twenties, also collecting and archiving his own maritime experiences and ship histories. His keen sense of authenticity has made him one of the most admired of American marine painters. Howard Barclay French was born in Fort Thomas, New York, and studied at the Arts Student League. French took over the work on this mural when Patterson died. He also produced many murals of ocean liners on display at the U.S. Merchant Marine Academy at Kings Point, New York. His work can also be found at the Peabody-Essex Museum in Salem, Massachusetts, and in archival issues of the periodical *Yachting*.
- To the left of the Perry flag as you face it is a mural jointly painted by French and Patterson of the USS *Hartford* and the Yacht *America*. Both these vessels served as training ships at the Academy.
- Moving counterclockwise around the room, you will approach a large mural on the Severn River side of Memorial Hall that depicts the opening action between the USS *Constitution* and the HMS *Java* in the War of 1812, painted by Patterson.
- To the right of the main door as you face it, is a painting of the USS *Delaware*. Her figurehead, carved to represent Tamanend, chief of the Delawares (a.k.a. Tecumseh), is on permenent display in the Visitor Center. This mural was painted by French.

- Just above the main door as you face it is a painting of the USS *Constellation* by Patterson. The *Constellation* was a training ship for the Naval Academy 1871–93 and is now a historic ship open to the public on the waterfront in Baltimore.
- To the left of the main door as you face it is a mural the USS *Monongahela* by French, briefly used as a Naval Academy training ship in 1894–97 and 1899.
- To the left of the *Monongahela* is another large mural that depicts the engagement between the USS *Constellation* and *L'Insurgente* in 1799 (during the American Revolution), painted by Patterson.
- To the right of the Perry flag is a depiction by French of the first salute to the Stars and Stripes by a foreign government in February 1778: a gun salute fired by the French Admiral La Motte Picquet to the *Ranger,* commanded by Capt. John Paul Jones in Quiberon Bay.

There are also two notable busts on either side of the Perry flag: to the left, one of Adm. William S. Benson, the first Chief of Naval Operations, sculpted by Jo Davidson; and, to the right, one of Rear Adm. Robley Dunglison Evans, Fleet Commander of the *Fort Fisher* in Valparaiso. Also on display are two historic flags: to the left as you enter Memorial Hall are the ensigns of the USS *South Dakota* (BB 57), and that of the USS *Ozbourn* (DD 846).

Architecturally, Memorial Hall is intended to be the apex and a dominant force in the Bancroft Hall complex. Ernest Flagg consciously designed the room in the traditions of Beaux-Arts principles—spatially along an axis of front to rear and bottom to top.[27] Beginning in 1998, a committee of alumni evaluated and redefined the criteria for memorialization and further restricted use of the Hall. It also directed extensive repairs and restoration. The committee's work was completed in 2003. While dances and other parties have been held in Memorial Hall in the past, recently enacted regulations have restored the room to more solemn commemorations.

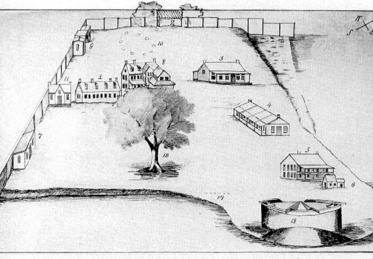

FORT SEVERN IN 1845 (FROM AN OLD MAP).
The numbers refer to the buildings, etc., as named after the Naval School was established.

achanan Row.	4. Apollo Row.	7. The Gas House.	10. Ring of Poplar Trees.	13. Fort Seve
he Abbey.	5. Rowdy Row.	8. Superintendent's House.	11. Chaplain's House.	14. Site of Pr
ess- and Recitation-Rooms.	6. Brandywine Cottage.	9. Gate-House.	12. Old Mulberry Tree.	

A Fort Severn map from 1845 marks where the "old mulberry tree" stood. *Courtesy Special Collections & Archives Division, Nimitz Library, U.S. Naval Academy*

THE OLD MULBERRY TREE
Outside the back of Bancroft Hall on either side of King Hall is Smoke Park, the outdoor place where midshipmen were allowed to have a cigarette. It was here (southwest of the site of Fort Severn) that a large mulberry tree stood for more than a century, until it was felled by a storm in the 1890s. For many years, the view from the Severn also included this friendly, natural navigation point.

DID YOU KNOW?
When the Civil War broke out, the Naval Academy was moved to Newport, Rhode Island, and the Yard was used as a hospital throughout the war. When the midshipmen students were given orders to head north to Newport, many from the South resigned to retreat to their home states. The gravity of their decision was not lost on the rest of the midshipmen, who were committed to defending the Union but who nonetheless had strong bonds with their Southern classmates.

In January, 1861, the highly popular number two man of the first class, Jardine G. Stone of Alabama, turned in his uniform and prepared to leave for his home in Mobile. Arm-in-arm with the class leader, William T. Sampson [for whom Sampson Hall, p. 46, is named], the honor man was escorted by his shipmates, singing their farewell song, to the gate. As they passed the quarters of the superintendent, Captain Blake, that officer appeared at his door. "What is the meaning of this rioting?" he demanded sternly. "It is no riot, sir," responded Sampson. "We are bidding our comrade farewell!" Blake stood silent for a moment. "Continue, gentlemen," he said, and abruptly returned indoors.[28]

The Yard was destroyed during the Civil War, with the brush completely eaten by cavalry horses, the lawn trodden by wagons, and various sheds built haphazardly on the parade grounds.[29]

SMOKE HALL ●

Below Memorial Hall (underneath the stairwell) is Smoke Hall, a light-filled and cavernous room that serves as an informal lounge for midshipmen. Four cases of historic flags and two figureheads adorn the walls and stairwells. Aptly named as the location where midshipmen were able to retreat for a cigarette, cigar, or pipe, Smoke Hall is an elegant receiving room and is also used for some

Smoke Hall, circa 1920. *Courtesy Special Collections & Archives Division, Nimitz Library, U.S. Naval Academy*

official functions. Smoking anywhere indoors has now been banned in the Yard and is also prohibited within ninety feet of a Federal building. Historically, it was strictly enforced: "One time President Grant, while visiting Admiral Porter, then superintendent, walked out with a friend for a short stroll smoking a cigar. A watchman approached and, not knowing the distinguished visitor, exclaimed, 'No smoking allowed on the grounds.' The President promptly destroyed the lighted cigar and congratulated the watchman for carrying out his orders."

KING HALL ●
Two staircases in the back of Smoke Hall lead down to the vast dining hall complex called King Hall, named after Fleet Adm. Ernest J. King, the Chief of Naval Operations from 1942–45. Covering more than 65,000 square feet of dining space, the hall hosts more than 12,000 meals a day to the hungry brigade. Like most of life in the Yard, mealtime is full of regimen and traditions.

Smoke Hall, as renovated in 2003, revealing one of the few Victorian-style ceilings in the Yard. *Courtesy Jamie Howren Photography*

Left: Dolphin sconces found throughout Smoke Hall. *Right:* The entrance from Smoke Hall into King Hall. *Courtesy Jamie Howren Photography*

Meals are served family style in King Hall for the entire brigade. King Hall is one of a few places in the Yard where the entire brigade can sit at once. Three minutes after the command "Brigade, Seats" is given, the entire brigade sits down in unison and the meal is hurriedly served. The cacophonic din can be overwhelming as more than 4,000 young people scramble to fill their stomachs.

On average, more than 1,100 gallons of milk and juice, two tons of meat, one ton of green vegetables, two tons of potatoes, 1,200 loaves of bread, and 720 pies are consumed daily. Two rotary-gas ovens cancook 200 twenty-pound turkeys at one time; six steam-jacketed kettles can cook 750 gallons of soup at a time; and the scullery handles more than 30,000 pieces of silverware, dishes, and glassware after each meal.

Industrial steam-jacketed kettles can cook 750 gallons of soup at a time. *Courtesy Jamie Howren Photography*

The doughnut machine in King Hall, capable of producing 10,000 doughnuts for the brigade. *Courtesy Jamie Howren Photography*

The mids' favorite meal? How about the Buffalo Chicken Sandwich and Flapsticks? The Buffalo Chicken Sandwich boasts a filling combination of a deep-fried, breaded chicken patty with blue cheese crumbles, lettuce and tomato, Frank's Hot Sauce mixed with mayo and cayenne pepper—all crammed in between a potato hamburger roll (untoasted). It is served with cheddar munchers (a potato/French-fry variation). What are Flapsticks? This staple is a sausage on a stick dipped in blueberry batter and baked. (Then, it is probably covered in butter and syrup.)

The mids' favorite dessert? An unscientific survey of several alumni from the 1990s reveals that "cannonballs and hard sauce" were the perennial favorite. As Cdr. John Mustin, Class of 1990, recalls, "It's like an apple turnover and the hard sauce is like cake icing, but thicker—extremely filling and fattening. The unwritten rule is that if a plebe can eat the whole table's cannonballs (twelve of them) and all of the hard sauce—it's a big vat of the stuff, then he gets to 'carry on'" ("carry on" means that the midshipman is dismissed and no longer has to stand or sit at attention). Good thing the brigade's daily regimen includes a lot of exercise!

King Hall is proud to serve homemade ice cream made on site daily. In the "ice cream room" it takes two people two days to make enough ice cream to serve two items to the entire brigade. This creamery tradition dates back to the days when the Academy had a dedicated dairy on Academy property, which was closed in 1998.

Once a year, King Hall hosts an end-of-summer crab feast, where they serve 210 bushels of steamed Chesapeake Bay blue crabs. They also host a Dark Ages Dinner, a feast held in the dead of winter. Each midshipman is delivered 1.5 pounds of choice lobster and beef tenderloin. On Thanksgiving, King Hall serves a traditional holiday meal that is offered to the extended Academy family—staff, faculty, and their families for only $5.85 per person.

In 2006, King Hall underwent extensive renovations, opening up the ceiling to skylights and taking the existing buttresses down to their original wood finish.

GHOST STORIES FROM THE YARD

"When I was plebe, I had been told that my grandfather's ghost walked the halls of Bancroft Hall and I've been told that since I was a child." Chris Kidd, Class of 1976, has a rich family legacy in the Navy and at the Naval Academy. His father and grandfather were graduates. Chris Kidd

---

DID YOU KNOW?
More than fifteen movies have featured the Yard or the Naval Academy, including the 1916 film Hero of Submarine D2 *and the 1991 film* Patriot Games, *starring Harrison Ford.*

---

was a humble plebe in 1972 when he started hearing the voices. "We would hear voices in Bancroft Hall where there shouldn't be voices, but they were murmuring voices—almost like a television that had been left on and then we would hear someone laugh. It would be a chuckle and you never quite knew what that was."

It was particularly spooky during "Windows" duty. "Windows" was a taxing job usually assigned to the plebes. Upperclassmen would leave their windows cracked for the fresh air, but would make the plebes run around in the middle of the night to shut each window, so that the upperclassmen would not have to wake up to frigid linoleum floors. Sometimes, when fulfilling his lonely nighttime duty, Chris Kidd discovered more than he expected. "As a plebe, you didn't wanna, like, hang around and look for [the source of the voices]. So, you would get these windows closed and you'd beat feet back to your room and you didn't care if you heard voices or not."

But he did care. He was perplexed. The noises seemed to come from within the walls of Bancroft Hall. And there was a space in Bancroft Hall he couldn't explain. Could that account for the voices?

When you looked inside the room, you could dimension it, but when you went outside the building and looked at it, the room should have been much, much bigger. So, it was clear that there was a void in the wall, a big void. To make a long story short, we removed the medicine cabinet, [the] stainless steel medicine cabinet, we unscrewed the medicine cabinet and pulled it out and inside was the equivalent of a room on the inside of this void.

Inside was a makeshift lounge, with bean bag chairs, a radio, old cigars, and old bottles. "So, what happened was, of course, each successive class very quietly passed on the fact that this secret room existed." One ghost story solved. But, there was more.

One day, Chris Kidd saw the ghost of Philo McGiffin, Class of 1882—or at least he thought he did. Philo McGiffin was a midshipman in the late 1870s, legendary for his practical jokes and pranks, the most famous of which alleges he rolled cannonballs down the passageways of the old dormitory in the Yard (before Bancroft Hall was built). Apparently, he kept a pyramid of old cannonballs dating back to 1812 in his room at the top of a set of stairs. One restless night, he decided to wake everyone up by rolling the cannonballs down the stairs. They wreaked havoc on the dormitory, tearing away banisters, bumping down steps and dropping into lower hallways. Midshipman McGiffin was sent to the prison ship, the *Santee*, to reflect on his misdeeds. While there, he made friends with the jailer and, when his sentence was served, he walked off the ship with gunpowder. He proceeded to load the gunpowder into the six big guns captured in the Mexican War that lay in the center of the Yard, and at midnight on 1 July, he fired a salute that woke the entire brigade and shattered many a window.

Many a midshipman over the years has reported sightings of the ghost of McGiffin rolling cannonballs through Bancroft Hall. But Chris Kidd swears he saw him one night outside.

> I was standing watch and was dispatched to carry
> an envelope up to Hospital Point. . . . It was 7:00
> or 8:00 o'clock at night and I [was carrying] the
> envelope. [In order to get to Hospital Point,]
> you would go down through Smoke Park and

THE TUNNELS

For as long as folklore has been circulating about the Naval Academy and the Yard, the "tunnels" have inspired tales. The tunnels refer to underground steam pipe tunnels that supposedly traverse beneath the Yard and, some will say, extend into downtown Annapolis. There are tall tales of midshipmen cavorting in the legendary tunnels: escaping the Yard for an anonymous night on the town, posting graffiti on the walls of the tunnels, stealing kisses with girls in the dripping heat, or playing late-night games in the haze and maze.

> He lifted the grating that covered the slanting steel ladder, slipped underneath, and then let it back down. He descended the ladder into a concrete pit that ended in a steel door. . . . He closed the door behind him and looked around. He was standing in a small vestibule facing the main passageway in a T-junction. He looked both ways down the tunnels. There were sixty-watt bulbs encased in steam-tight globes every twenty feet, and their yellow light seemed to accentuate the subterranean atmosphere. The only bare concrete visible was on the floor, as the sides and the overhead were covered by cable bundles, various-sized conduits, water pipes, and thickly lagged steam pipes. There was a hum of electricity in the air, audible against a background of hissing steam and the occasional clank of thermal expansion in the pipes. The air was humid and smelled of ozone and old pipe lagging. The pipes were marked at intervals with their contents and pressures. A ribbon of corrugated steel deck plates ran down the center of the five-foot-wide floor, under which ran the main sewage-pumping system.[30]

Do they exist? Are they large enough for humans to run around? Do they allow midshipmen to escape the confines of the Yard without exiting through the gates? You decide. . . .

would cross over the bridge like you were going to the obstacle course. . . . Undoubtedly, Philo McGiffin was there standing next to a gun and, as I crossed the bridge, the gun fired and there's no explanation for the fact that the gun fired.

McGiffin was standing in turn-of-the-century midshipmen dress—full dress blues with buttons all the way up and a pillbox cap. And the gun fired? "The gun fired."

When you are back outside Bancroft Hall, head toward Tecumseh and take a left onto the red brick walkway outside the courtyard. About a block's distance by foot is Dahlgren Hall, our next stop—but stop briefly to look at the two monuments at the corner of Buchanan and Blake roads, the Centennial monument to the U.S. submarine force and the Midway Monument.

CENTENNIAL MONUMENT TO THE U.S. SUBMARINE FORCE

A dark, polished granite monument commemorates the contributions submarines and their crews have made between 1900 and 2000. Notice the ghostly human faces and dolphins etched in the waves. Unusual for an Academy monument is the fact that the corporate donors who helped to commission it are listed on this monument. The sculptor is Paul Wegner, the same artist who produced the bust of Adm. Hyman G. Rickover, Class of 1922, in Rickover Hall

MIDWAY MONUMENT

To the right of the Submarine Force Monument is the Battle of Midway Monument, which chronicles the story of the battle that turned the tide of the Pacific theater during World War II and pays tribute to the service members

The Centennial Monument. *Courtesy U.S. Naval Academy Photographic Services*

The annual wreath-laying ceremony at the Midway Monument. *Courtesy U.S. Naval Academy Photographic Services*

who played a critical role in this battle's victory over the Japanese. Along the paved walkway leading to the monument are two additional, smaller granite structures that outline the losses suffered in the battle.

This passageway, with a heavy Asian architectural influence, connects Bancroft Hall to Dahlgren Hall. A symmetrical passageway connects Bancroft Hall to the Natatorium. *Courtesy Jamie Howren Photography*

DAHLGREN HALL

As you approach the façade of Dahlgren Hall, note its resemblance to old European train stations, with its vast, shed-like appearance.

Indeed, as part of the original Flagg-designed group of buildings, Dahlgren Hall reflects the École des Beaux-Arts training Flagg received in France. Dahlgren (originally an armory used for storing the midshipmen's training weaponry) and Macdonough (originally a gymnasium) halls were designed to flank Bancroft Hall symmetrically and evoke images of a fortified gate, a common theme of French classicism. Symbolically, they were intended to represent the military and naval functions of the Academy. In between the granite piers of each tower is enclosed a monumental arched opening of masonry, metal, and glass. The metal grill was painted green with ornamental terracotta tiles as infill.[31] It shows the beginning of Art Deco influence with its individual *and* decorative images enmeshed.

This armory housed the midshipmen's rifles and shipboard guns and was used for training. In addition, the cavernous interior and spacious center provided an ideal venue for ceremonial and sporting events. President Theodore Roosevelt spoke here on 24 April 1906, at the historic ceremony celebrating the return of John Paul Jones's remains in the Yard.

View of Dahlgren Hall from the Chapel, circa 1906.
Courtesy Special Collections & Archives Division, Nimitz Library, U.S. Naval Academy

Cannons housed in the Academy's Armory (now Dahlgren Hall), circa 1865–81. *Courtesy Special Collections & Archives Division, Nimitz Library, U.S. Naval Academy*

The entrance into Dahlgren Hall with the reflection of the Chapel dome in the glass. *Courtesy Jamie Howren Photography*

Dahlgren Hall's history is quite storied and the building is chock full of Naval Academy and Navy memorabilia. Named for Rear Adm. John A. Dahlgren, a prolific ordnance inventor who designed a variety of guns—such as the Dahlgren rifle and the Dahlgren thirty-pounder—the building houses his bust at the foot of the stairs leading down to the Dry Dock Restaurant. If you turn around and look back up above the front entrance doors, you will also notice a sizeable oil portrait of Rear Admiral Dahlgren, painted by Leslie Cotton in the nineteenth century.

The towering arc of the interior of the building is supported by bronze buttresses that are dotted with lights, giving the interior of the building a holiday

Rear Adm. John A. Dahlgren. *Courtesy Special Collections & Archives Division, Nimitz Library, U.S. Naval Academy*

glow year round. The rear window is partly obscured by a model tall ship that is suspended from the wall, a model of the USS *Antietam*, constructed in 1876 for the American Centennial Exposition in Philadelphia. It was used in Dahlgren Hall as a teaching tool for midshipmen to learn how to work the rigging of a ship. It was restored by the Elizabeth S. Hooper Foundation and the Class of 1951. State flags provided by the Daughters of the American Revolution line the sides, as do numerous bronze plaques commemorating various naval officers who died in combat or in the line of duty.

Since 1903, Dahlgren Hall has also served as the official venue for "hops," the official dances hosted by the brigade. The tradition was festive: "The great hall is lighted by globes suspended high overhead, but not brilliantly lighted; for some dances, indeed, the lights are dimmed low. The decorative scheme varies with the energies and ingenuity of the Hop Committee, but it nearly always includes pillars of bunting, illumined from below, that shed a mystical and colorful glow over the scene."[32]

The annual Ring Dance, where second-class midshipmen (juniors) receive their school rings, was a highlight.

> There is one hop of the year about which traditions have been growing and over which, more than any other dance—with the possible exception of the June Ball—the aura of sentiment hovers. That is the Ring Hop. [It] has grown out of the sentiment attached to the ring, one of the most treasured of all a graduate's possessions. . . . [T]he crowning event of the evening arrives when each couple mounts the carpeted dias and passes through the large gilded replica of the class ring, surmounted by a glowing globe of crystals that simulates the jewel.[33]

The midshipman's ring is worn like a necklace on ribbon that night and is "christened" by being dipped into a bowl that contains water from each of the seven seas (literally) and from the Severn River to remind midshipmen of the four years they are spending together by the Bay "where the Severn joins the sea."

In recent years, the annual Ring Dance is held on Radford Terrace between Michelson and Chauvenet halls or on Forrest Sherman Field. Dahlgren Hall now serves as a student union, activity center and lounge, with a cafeteria-style restaurant, the Dry Dock (open to the public seven days a week, 8 AM–10 AM—except for June, when it is open Monday–Friday, 8 AM–3 PM and Saturday–Sunday, 10 AM–5 PM), couches and coffee tables for relaxation, public restrooms, and even an ATM. Private, catered

An artist's rendition of Dahlgren Hall, before it was built, predicting its seasonal use as an ice hockey and ice skating rink. *Courtesy Special Collections & Archives Division, Nimitz Library, U.S. Naval Academy*

events are also held in the lounge space on the upper level. The large area on the first level was used for ice hockey games and winter ice skating from 1974 to 2006.

Other items to note on the walls inside Dahlgren Hall:

- Marble portrait bust of Rear Adm. Dahlgren, by Theodore Mills, 1970;
- USS *Olympia* stern ornaments by Alvan C. Nye, circa 1900, transferred from Norfolk Navy Yard in 1920;
- "Winged Victory" bronze gun turret ornament from the USS *Massachusetts,* bronze gun turret ornament from the USS *Alabama,* and bronze gun turret from the USS *Kearsarge,* all created by Bela L. Pratt, and all three were transferred from the Philadelphia Navy Yard between 1919 and 1921;
- "Figure of Hope" bronze gun turret ornament from the USS *Rhode Island,* also by Bela Pratt, and transferred from the Mare Island Navy Yard in 1922;
- Wooden USS *Macedonian* and USS *Trenton* sternboards.

As you step back outside, you will notice a collection of guns and cannons scattered in the grassy area in front of Dahlgren. It is called the Dahlgren "gun park"—a fitting place given Rear Admiral Dahlgren's prominence in the field of ordnance. Placed in the gun park are:

- One of two Japanese torpedoes in the Dahlgren gun park is this Type 93, the largest enemy weapon encountered in World War II, which carried 1,000 pounds of explosives and could travel a range of approximately 30,000 yards at forty knots. It was acquired by the Naval Academy in 1946 through the efforts of Capt. R. M. Fortson, USNR.

HISTORIC MARKERS
Like the plaques in front of the Administration Building,
two ground markers in front of Dahlgren Hall identify the
site of old residential quarters.

- This aerial torpedo, a Type 91, was delivered to the Academy in October 1945. It was painted to match other ordnance on display in the area.
- The 75-mm howitzer was captured with its gun crew in August 1944 by the 8th Naval Beach Battalion and the 540th Army Engineers at St. Raphael on the French Riviera. Germans used this gun to prevent the Allied invasion of southern France.
- Two identical Hotchkiss guns were captured during the Battle of Santiago Bay, Cuba, in 1898 and donated to the Academy.
- The Dahlgren rifle (cannon) is one of Rear Admiral Dahlgren's most famous inventions. Experts believe this one is an experimental model and that the plaque and identification are erroneous. It has the smoothbore form that Dahlgren traditionally used, but is considered

This Japanese Type 93 torpedo from World War II can be found in the Dahlgren gun park, a grassy area in front of Dahlgren hall.
Courtesy Jamie Howren Photography

to be too small for a service shell gun. Investigators who examined the gun in the 1960s found the bore was already plugged and paint had covered up one digit of the markings on the left side.

From Dahlgren Hall, head toward Porter Road and back in the general direction of the Visitor Center. Along the way, we'll point out the buildings you will pass.

The B-1 Wright biplane on its makeshift landing strip next to Dahlgren Hall in 1911, surrounded by curious bystanders.
Courtesy Special Collections & Archives Division, Nimitz Library, U.S. Naval Academy

---

DID YOU KNOW?
Lt. John Rodgers, Class of 1903, naval aviator #2, delivered, assembled, and flew a B-1 Wright biplane above and around the Yard on 7 September 1911. It took off and landed on Farragut Field—right in front of Dahlgren Hall.

WARD HALL ⊖

As you walk along Buchanan Road, you will pass by Ward Hall, a neoclassical structure built in 1941 for the Ordnance or Weapons Department. The building's namesake, Cdr. James Harmon Ward, was the first commandant and the first professor of naval gunnery at the Naval Academy. Ward was also the first Union naval officer killed in the Civil War. Ward Hall now houses the Academy's Department of Information Technology.

At the end of Buchanan Road, you will be facing Porter Road. In front of you is a tree-lined street of gracious homes with screened front porches. This is where the senior officers assigned to work at the Naval Academy live with their families. (There are other living quarters on Upshur and Rodgers roads. They line the edge of Worden Field, which you can see on your way to visit the cemetery (see page 150).

Turn left onto Porter Road and meander down the street to get a closer look at the residences.

Left: The entrance to Ward Hall. *Courtesy Jamie Howren Photography. Right:* Cdr. James H. Ward. *Courtesy Special Collections & Archives Division, Nimitz Library, U.S. Naval Academy*

RESIDENCES IN THE YARD ●

The official residences of the faculty and staff on Porter Road and the homes on the perimeter of Worden Field (Upshur and Rodgers roads) are historically significant as physical structures, but they also carry cherished memories for the families assigned to live there, playing a large role in the culture of the Yard. Living on a college campus creates an easy commute for the officers, professors, and staff who work at the Naval Academy. For the families, it means living in a scenic, safe, and meticulously maintained community with park amenities: tennis courts, sailboats, and walking paths.

The homes on Porter, Upshur, and Rodgers roads are much larger than most officers' quarters on military bases around the world, which can be both a blessing and a curse. Residents assigned to these homes are afforded elegant and cavernous living and entertaining spaces, but these structures and their grounds require extensive maintenance and cleaning. They boast wraparound porches, formal entryways, intricate woodwork, sixteen-foot ceilings, and four thousand square feet of living space. Built in the Victorian era, they were designed to accommodate extended family (grandparents) and live-in help, which was more common then for the middle class.

But these homes were not always as big and elegant. In the late 1800s, it became evident (and embarrassing) that the Academy could not adequately house its staff and faculty on the grounds. It was common at the time for the residents in the Yard to keep chickens and cows in their back yards and the flow of raw sewage from the older residences near the old Fort Severn became a protracted problem. The refuse was allegedly running through the streets of the Yard into the Severn River.

So, as part of the master plan for the "New Academy," Ernest Flagg was hired to redesign "Captains Row" along

Porter Road, including the superintendent's new quarters. A canal was actually dug in front of the homes to ferry building materials to the Chapel construction site.

Inside, the homes boast marble fireplaces with ornately carved mantles, brass doorknobs cast with the Naval Academy crest, eleven-foot ceilings, and open staircases that wrap upward three stories. The original kitchens were in the basement, replete with dumbwaiters to send food up to the dining rooms on the main floor (most of the dumbwaiters are still installed).

Kim Anderson was twelve years old when her family lived at #3 Porter Road in the 1970s, right on a corner, and she liked hanging out in her home's dumbwaiter. The Yard was a paradise of fun for a young girl, with a full neighborhood of other kids to play with, an ice-skating rink at Dahlgren Hall, and tennis courts. One midshipman nicknamed "Doc" adopted Kim as a type of little sister and used to serenade her when his squad marched past her house. One day during plebe summer (when the plebes train prior to the start of the school year), he had them sing, "We love you, Kimmie! Oh yes, we do!" As Kim described it, "I wasn't there to hear the serenade, but my dad was home sick. He came out in his pajamas and Doc was quite embarrassed."

BILL THE GOAT

At the intersection of Porter Road and Cooper Road are several monuments, including a bronze replica of the Naval Academy's mascot, Bill the Goat. A live goat first

---

DID YOU KNOW?
Mark Twain, a.k.a. Samuel Clemens, was a visitor to 29 Upshur Road in 1907. He was invited to watch a special midshipmen parade as a guest of then-Superintendent Rear Adm. James H. Sands.

"Bill the Goat" in 1925. *Courtesy Special Collections & Archives Division, Nimitz Library, U.S. Naval Academy*

Bronze replica of Bill the Goat. *Courtesy Jamie Howren Photography*

PAYING CALLS
One long-standing custom no longer practiced in the
Yard was the Saturday ritual of "paying calls," the
obligatory social requirement for new families moving
into the Yard at the turn of the twentieth century. Officers
and their families were expected to visit each home in
the Yard and leave calling cards as proof of their visit.
Men were required to leave two cards, one for both the
gentleman and the lady of the house, and women were
required to leave one card. If children accompanied
them, the corners of the cards were turned down.

made a debut as an accidental Navy mascot in 1893 when
the USS *New York* made a port visit to Annapolis and the
ship's own goat mascot, named "El Cid," was brought to
the Army-Navy football game. Navy won the game and
the midshipmen were convinced that the goat played a
role in their victory.

In the early twentieth century, the goat became
known as "Bill," a name borrowed from a pet goat owned
by the Commandant of Midshipmen at the time. The

Statue of Bill the Goat and Lejeune Hall, the home of the Naval
Academy Athletic Hall of Fame. *Courtesy Jamie Howren
Photography*

Academy has kept a goat mascot ever since. Bill now parades through the home games.

This bronze statue, donated by the Class of 1915 in 1957, was sculpted by Clemente Spampinato, an Italian-born sculptor known for his sports- and western-themed sculptures. He has been admired for his ability to bring his subjects to life by representing them in complex movement. In addition to Bill, he created the Bobby Jones sculpture on display at the World Golf Hall of Fame in Pinehurst, North Carolina.

LEJEUNE HALL

The statue of Maj. Gen. John Archer Lejeune, the thirteenth Commandant of the Marine Corps and member of the Class of 1888, stands guard outside his namesake building. This sculpture was created by Louisiana artist Patrick Miller, who also created Lejeune likenesses for Lejeune's hometown of New Roads, Louisiana; Camp Lejeune in North Carolina; Marine Corps Base, Quantico,

Virginia; and the new Marine Corps Heritage Museum, also in Quantico, Virginia. There is one other full statue in the Yard, that of Commodore George H. Perkins, on the terrace outside Memorial Hall.

Statue of Lt. Gen.
John A. Lejeune.
*Courtesy Jamie
Howren Photography*

Opened in 1982, Lejeune Hall is the first building in the Yard named for a Marine. A 95,000-square-foot steel, granite, concrete, and glass athletic facility, it was built on land that was originally used as a football field, Thompson Field. Its mansard roof and granite walls are intended to complement the other contemporary buildings and the Flagg complex of buildings. It also houses two swimming pools, multiple wrestling rings, and the Naval Academy Athletic Hall of Fame. A plaque about Thompson Field and its namesake is located on the King George Street side of the building. Now Academy football games and other major outdoor athletic events are played in Navy-Marine Corps Memorial Stadium (see section Outside the Yard). You can visit the Athletic Hall of Fame on the second floor of Lejeune Hall, which houses several bowl game trophies.

THOMPSON FIELD ROCK

Just below the entrance of Lejeune Hall (on the left side of the ramp as you face the front of the building) is a large rock that doesn't appear to fit in with the natural landscape. This boulder was placed here as a memorial to all those who died in World War II. Under it is a time capsule containing memorabilia from the Class of 1940, the alumni who dedicated it. The time capsule is to be opened by the Class of 2040. Turn left onto King George Street and head back toward the Visitor Center.

HALSEY FIELD HOUSE

On the right side of King George Street is the Halsey Field House, which was built in 1957 and named after Fleet Adm. William F. Halsey, Class of 1904, Commander of the Third Fleet in World War II. The concrete building is seventy feet tall and has no vertical support. Built to house the growing athletic activities of the brigade, it has an indoor track, multipurpose gymnasiums, and even a climbing wall (for midshipmen's use). An Art Deco frieze entitled "The Athlete" adorns the façade of the building.

Just beyond Halsey Field House is the Visitor Center—where you started. You can finish your Yard tour now or head out for a perimeter tour. This extended visit will take you on a hike along the edge of the Chesapeake Bay and Severn River, giving you an opportunity to see some historic sights on the far perimeter of the Yard, including the Cemetery and some of the more contemporary structures in the Yard.

PART II *The perimeter*

The perimeter

As you exit the Visitor Center to begin the "outer" or perimeter tour, you will be facing the water with a red-brick sidewalk in front of you. Look behind you and see the Naval Academy crest on the front of the Center. Adopted as the official Navy coat of arms in 1898, it was designed by Park Benjamin, Class of 1867, a philanthropist and businessman, and approved by the Secretary of the Navy in 1899. It depicts a hand grasping a trident. Below is a shield bearing a Roman galley that is moving forward; below that is an open book and the Academy's motto: "Ex Scientia Tridens," or "From knowledge, sea power." You will notice this seal is used all over the Yard on building façades, in the embedded compass rose in front of Tecumseh, and even on some doorknobs.

The Sea Wall, as it looked in 1890. *Courtesy Special Collections & Archives Division, Nimitz Library, U.S. Naval Academy*

RUNNING IN THE YARD

"There are two primary routes, known affectionately as an 'inner' and an 'outer,' referring to the inner perimeter and outer perimeter of the Yard," explains Cdr. John Mustin, USNR, Class of 1990. "An inner is approximately three miles—what I typically did—and an outer is about five miles and was favored by the crew team and SEAL and Marine Corps wannabees. . . . I also liked to run 'the rocks,' meaning the quay wall on the seawall. . . . It takes agility and various leg muscles; you work different leg muscles each time you run it. But it's only a few hundred yards, so you don't kill yourself when you run. It's also a good start to an 'inner' or an 'outer.' Those are the rocks that face over to town, so you also get a good view of the boats coming and going from the marina, and also the ones featured in A Sense of Honor. . . . You always had to be careful of the slime that grew on the rocks, since they were slippery when wet."

The Yard is open for recreational runners who bring valid identification (i.e., a driver's license), but headphones are not allowed.

COMPASS ROSE PLAZA

As you follow the sidewalk, it will curve with the shoreline. Many Naval Academy classes and other donor groups have found this picturesque setting a fitting location for class gifts—for example, benches, monuments, fountains. The first one you approach is the Compass Rose Plaza, dedicated by the Class of 1943. To the left of the walkway is a building with an angular wall of windows facing the water, Ricketts Hall.

RICKETTS HALL

Ricketts Hall is named after Adm. Claude Vernon Ricketts, former Vice Chief of Naval Operations and Class of 1929. Its waterfront façade is intended to evoke the image of the superstructure of a ship.[34] This building, finished in 1966 and originally used to house enlisted

personnel assigned to the Academy, was completely renovated in 1995. The three-story, 78,000-square-foot building now serves as offices for the Naval Academy Athletic
Association, offering state-of-the-art fitness and training
facilities, lockers, and storage for Navy athletic teams.

The fitness facility alone is 9,000 square feet big, with
a forty-yard running track down the middle. The architects from CSD in Baltimore determined that the brigade's

Ricketts Hall. *Courtesy Jamie Howren Photography*

highly regimented schedule can result in a large portion
of the men and women hitting the gym at the same time,
which necessitated a plan for a workout facility much
larger than would normally be built on a college campus.

RIP MILLER FIELD
Just next to Ricketts Hall is Rip Miller Field, a turf
field named after a beloved football coach and Assistant
Director of Athletics at the Naval Academy from 1931 to
74. Edgar E. "Rip" Miller was inducted into the National

Football Foundation Hall of Fame in 1966. The Heisman trophies awarded to Joseph Bellino, Class of 1961, and Roger Staubach, Class of 1965, are on display on the seaward side.

The Sea Wall, along the Chesapeake Bay. *Courtesy Jamie Howren Photography*

THE SEA WALL

As the sidewalk ends, you will notice a wall of jagged rocks, stone coping that was part of a wall that surrounded the State House in downtown Annapolis, which the Academy purchased from the State of Maryland in the late 1800s. This is the official start of the storied "Sea Wall." It is the Academy's window to the outside world. Lightly buffered from the elements, Bancroft Hall is protected from high waves by this low formation of randomly placed and various-sized boulders. It has found its place in a famous novel by James Webb about the Naval Academy entitled *A Sense of Honor*:

> The seawall made a dark crisp line below the whiteness of the Chesapeake Bay, just across the

road from Farragut Field. Fogarty ran it every morning, hundreds of large, flat stones piled on top of each other, each one four or five feet around, each one angled in a different way, so that anyone trying to run the wall would have to hop from rock to rock, rather than merely going in a straight line. Most of the rocks were covered with ice or moss.

Fogarty never ran the sea wall until he was tired. He used it as a test, a game that pitted his fear against his courage. One wrong step, or one unlucky one, and he would fall, smashing his body onto wide, sharp rocks that could easily break his bones or crack his skull. But that was all a part of it.

He reached the wall. The icy confluence of river and sea surged along the lower rocks, ice scraping up at him with swells from the distant sea, sounding something like rats gnawing wood. . . . Fogarty chanted as he jogged, in a mindless, repetitive whisper. "I can run all night. . . . I can run all day. . . . I can run all night."[35]

The windswept path along the Sea Wall is popular for painters, lovers and loiterers. The scenery is the best the Chesapeake Bay has to offer. As you walk along, take time to notice the many sea-related memorials and monuments.

HARTFORD POINT LIGHT

Dedicated in honor of Adm. David Farragut's flagship in the Battle of Mobile Bay, this painted cast-iron light post from the USS *Hartford* was placed here in 1959.

THE USS *MAINE* FOREMAST

The USS *Maine* is known as the "longest ship in the world" since the ship's foremast is located here and the

The foremast to the USS *Maine. Courtesy Jamie Howren Photography*

ship's mainmast is located at Arlington National Cemetery, approximately seventy-five miles away. The USS *Maine*, a battleship that was blown up in Havana Harbor in Cuba in 1898, was recovered from the harbor in 1910 and placed in the Yard in 1913.

The Sea Gate. *Courtesy Jamie Howren Photography*

THE SEA GATE

Just past the *Maine* mast is a set of stairs that leads into the bay. These stairs are known as the Sea Gate and provide a permanent landing for sailboats and a seaward entry to the Academy. But, for some midshipmen, it is a place of reflection. Liz Yatko, Class of 2004, says, "One of my favorite places is the Sea Gate, with the steps to the water. They feel like a step out to the future. I go there when I need to think things through."

THE *PADDLE* BELL

The ship's bell from the USS *Paddle* has been placed here as a reminder of the toll of the loss of American submarines during World War II. Another monument to the lost submarines USS *Thresher* and USS *Scorpion* is located in the Nimitz Library (see page 142).

THE WORLD WAR II SUBMARINER MEMORIAL

The "Courage Runs Deep" monument is a memorial to the 3,505 men (374 officers and 3,131 enlisted sailors) who lost their lives on fifty-two submarines during World War

The "Courage Runs Deep" Monument. *Courtesy Jamie Howren Photography*

II. The ten-foot steel torpedo is a Mark XIV type, the main armament used in World War II submarines. The Submarine Bicentennial Commission offered a submarine medal to raise funds for this memorial, dedicated in 1976.

THE *TRITON* LIGHT

Sitting at the intersection of the Severn River and the Chesapeake Bay—at the very edge of the Yard—is a beacon called the *Triton* Light. It is the only navigational light in the Yard and is dedicated to the safe return of all those who go out to sea on ships. It contains water samples collected from twenty-two seas by the USS *Triton* (SSRN-586) in 1960 when it conducted the first submerged circumnavigation of the world. Every design element was chosen to be highly symbolic. Its three sides

The *Triton* Light. *Courtesy Jamie Howren Photography*

show three facets of a sailor's life: God, Country, Ship. It rests on landfill, or "new soil"—representing the growth of the Navy. The rough finish of the base and the smooth finish of the pedestal denote the rigors of life at sea and the satisfaction of the career. The bronze shaft is emblematic of the permanence of naval traditions; the Art Deco-style lattice work on the shaft symbolizes how technology can adapt these long-held traditions.

Continue straight ahead to visit the Robert Crown Sailing Center, the headquarters for Navy Sailing and the Naval Academy's sea-based training.

ROBERT CROWN SAILING CENTER ⬤

As you reach the end of the Sea Wall, off to the left you'll notice a small harbor in front of you. This is the Santee Basin, the location that has historically served as the debarkation point for Navy Sailing. It was named after the *Santee*, a ship that was berthed at the Naval Academy dock in Annapolis from 1863 until she sank at her wharf in 1912. The *Santee* was replaced by the *Reina Mercedes,* a Spanish naval ship captured during the Spanish-American War. Both the *Santee* and the *Reina Mercedes* were assigned several functions during their tenure in the Yard, including housing for enlisted Naval Academy personnel and even as a brig, or jail. They served as the permanent center of waterfront activity for the next forty-five years.[36]

Class of 1921 graduate Capt. David Harvey Byerly remembers a short imprisonment while a midshipman, "My second month at the Academy, I was caught smoking in the bathroom. I ended up in the *Reina Mercedes* for two weeks." It did not deter him from smoking in the bathroom but, from then on, he did ensure that he snuck a cigarette when there was an "outboard tendency," or when the wind was blowing *out* the window of his room. In 1957, the *Reina Mercedes* was replaced with a small,

The Santee Basin view of the Robert Crown Center. *Courtesy U.S. Naval Academy Photographic Services*

one-story building, a flimsy headquarters for Navy Sailing. As veteran Navy sailor Ed Cotter, Class of 1973, described it, "It was [actually] a double-wide trailer—a shed with a couple of desks and a chalkboard. . . . Back then, the program was all done on a shoestring and it was all informal." The structure was considered woefully inadequate—especially when a visiting sloop poked its bowsprit through an outboard wall directly above one of the secretary's desks!

So, a group of former Navy sailors and then-Superintendent Vice Adm. James F. Calvert, Class of 1943, lobbied Congress and private sources to fund the construction of a fitting headquarters for Navy Sailing. It was designed by Ellerbe Becket of Bloomington, Minnesota, an architectural firm that also designed several of the buildings at the Mayo Clinic.

Perched at the edge of the Basin, the Crown Center is one of the more modern pieces of architecture in the Yard. Named in honor of Capt. Robert Crown, USNR,

The front view of the Robert Crown Center. *Courtesy U.S. Naval Academy Photographic Services*

the building was dedicated in the spring of 1974 and later renovated in 2004. Captain Crown, a former president of the Navy League of the United States, was twice awarded the Secretary of the Navy's Distinguished Public Service Award for his tireless dedication to the Navy as a civilian.

With a structure that looks like a mast and sail, it appears as if it is ready to get underway. Angular lines, like those of a mast, and triangular shapes, like those of a

---

DID YOU KNOW?
The Robert Crown Sailing Center houses the Intercollegiate Sailing Hall of Fame trophies and memorabilia on the second floor of the Center.

---

sail, are repeated throughout, but a copper roof complements and provides some consistency with the Flagg-designed architecture so prominent in the central part of the Yard. Its windows soar seaward, reflecting in its panes the Academy's training vessels moored nearby along the Santee Basin seawall.

This is the center of activity for Navy sailing and, more importantly, the cornerstone of professional development for the midshipmen. In fact, the Academy considers sailing a "crucible" for leadership training. The program, housed here at the Crown Center, provides challenging opportunities for these naval officers-in-training to master small-boat handling, navigation, safety at sea, watch standing, and small-unit leadership. Rear Adm. Robert McNitt, Class of 1938, an avid and accomplished sailor who has been closely involved with the Academy's sailing program for several decades, emphasizes, "This is the only thing we do here that reflects our mission. . . . It defines us as a maritime institution."

As you leave the Sailing Center and cross the parking lot, you will notice the training sailboats in the Santee Basin to your right. Continue walking with the Santee Basin on your right, cross Santee Road and continue on Brownson Road for about a block to reach the Levy Center, which includes the Academy's Jewish Chapel.

COMMODORE URIAH P. LEVY CENTER

The Commodore Uriah P. Levy Center, completed in 2005, is the newest addition to the Yard. Its design is intended to blend old and new, complementing the adjacent Bancroft Hall with its whitewashed limestone and many of the same horizontal lines so prevalent in the Flagg-designed, Beaux-Arts–style buildings. Its placement

WHAT'S A "YP"?
A small fleet of miniature ships, called "Yard Patrol" craft, or "YPs," is housed near the Academy and is used to teach ship handling and navigation, as well as better prepare the midshipmen for their future as naval officers. The ships are each 108 feet long, have twin screws, and are moored across the Severn River at the Naval Station Annapolis.

The Commodore Uriah P. Levy Center. *Photo © Alan Kachmacher. Courtesy Boggs & Partners Architects*

in the Yard at the nexus of King Hall, the seventh and eighth wings of Bancroft Hall, and an athletic field ensures that it is a highly trafficked path for midshipmen.

By locating the Levy Center on the opposite side of Farragut Field from the Sea Wall (along Brownson Road, parallel to Turner Joy Road), it was the architect's and the donors' hope that it will give midshipmen pause to reflect, to meditate, to pray, and to find their individual and collective center. (To visit the inside of the Levy Center, you will have to walk around Farragut Field.)

The Naval Academy was the last service academy to have a dedicated Jewish chapel. Named in honor of one of the most famous Jewish military officers (whose full-length portrait is hanging in the lobby of Preble Hall), the Commodore Uriah P. Levy Center and Jewish Chapel house more than just a brigade synagogue. It is also a dedicated training center for the moral development and education of the Brigade of Midshipmen.

As you step closer to the portico, you will notice it is vaguely classical in architectural style. Indeed, the portico is specifically intended to remind visitors of Monticello, the historic home of President Thomas Jefferson. It has seven entrances to welcome visitors as a reminder of Abraham's tent, which also had seven entrances, to emphasize inclusion. Commodore Levy admired Jefferson's advocacy of religious freedom and, when Jefferson's descendants could not afford to maintain Monticello, he purchased the property, rescuing it from its sure deterioration and restoring it to its original state. The Levy family eventually sold the property to the Jefferson Memorial Foundation in 1923.

When you step inside the atrium and look upward, you will notice the stunning mosaic dome in the shape of a double helix. The stone you see in the mosaic and throughout the building is ancient Jerusalem stone imported from a quarry near Hebron. The oculus is a pin-point view of the sky, a glimpse at the heavens before you enter a heavenly place.

The atrium boasts a Jerusalem stone, double-helix mosaic on the floor and a domed, prism skylight in the shape of the Star of David. *Photo © Alan Kachmacher. Courtesy Boggs & Partners Architects*

The Jewish Chapel is off to your right—a modern structure surrounded by ancient stone. It resembles a ship—with its hull-like shape, a towering mess scrim and an ethereal, silver-leaf ceiling. Behind the heavy glass doors are several quotes from Levy etched in the glass partitions. Perhaps the most notable: "I will by my deeds make it easier for those who come after and would serve as I serve." Commodore Levy was responsible for the elimination of "flogging," or corporal punishment, in the U. S. Navy.

The Jewish Chapel. *Photo © Alan Kachmacher. Courtesy Boggs & Partners Architects*

DID YOU KNOW?
In front of the Levy Center is a fountain with quotes from President John F. Kennedy, John Paul Jones, and members of the Class of 1960 etched on its three sides.

In the area where the Levy Center now stands, another fountain stood in front of Mitscher Hall, named for aviation pioneer and World War II hero Marc A. Mitscher, Class of 1910. Prior to the construction of the Levy Center, Mitscher Hall housed the Academy's All-Faiths Chapel and chaplains' offices. The fountain, or reflecting pool, was part of the building's air conditioning system but was most popular with the midshipmen for post-ceremony dunking and general frivolity. "We were splashing around in the fountain late one night," said Mackie Christenson, wife of Rear Adm. Ron Christenson, Class of 1969. "Suddenly, we realized there were two other couples splashing around, too! We didn't initially see them—you could literally hide under the fountain of water." The fountain was filled in when Mitscher Hall was hooked in the central chilled water system.

A forty-five-foot altar—again made of the Jerusalem stone—is inspired by the Western wall with a Sephardic arc that holds a Torah donated by the Israeli Navy. Above it is an eternal flame and on either side are the Ten Commandments, inscribed in an ancient form of Hebrew. The Naval Academy Chapel has been a fixture in the Yard and a place of solace, reflection and prayer for many midshipmen—Christian and non-Christian—for many years. The Levy Center and its Chapel now serve as another resource for midshipmen to reflect and renew in the Yard.

Once you leave the Levy Center, backtrack along Brownson Road toward the Sailing Center and take a left onto Santee Road. Head toward the dome in the distance—the entrance to the new soccer stadium. Before you reach the soccer stadium, you will see the backside of Luce Hall on your left. At the far end of the long row of parking spaces is the fifth wing of Bancroft Hall and the site of the old Fort Severn.

FORT SEVERN MARKER

Embedded on the side of the building is a plaque that marks the site of Fort Severn battery, the Yard's historical cornerstone and the first building in the Yard. Erected in 1808, the fort consisted of a fourteen-foot-high stone wall that enclosed a battery one hundred feet in diameter. Inside the wall was a magazine of brick with a small conical roof and eight guns mounted on a platform that ran between the wall and the magazine, allowing a 360-degree vantage point. A small parapet topped with sod rose above the platform. As the Naval Academy grew in size and increased in its number of buildings, the old navigation point became dwarfed by comparison. It was demolished in 1909.[37]

GLENN WARNER SOCCER FACILITY ●

Directly ahead and off to the right you will notice a building with a dome-shaped roof at the corner of Dewey Field. This is the entrance to the Warner soccer stadium, designed by CSD Architects, Baltimore, and completed in 2001. It was built on reclaimed land and is named for Glenn Warner, Academy soccer coach, 1946–75.

Inside the dome is also housed the Anders Hall of Honor, with tributes to many legendary Navy soccer players. The Anders Hall is named for father and son Cdr. Arthur F. Anders, Class of 1927, and Maj. Gen. William

---

HISTORIC MARKER
As you approach the Glen Warner Soccer Facility on your right, you will notice a marker on a pole on your left. This marks the spot where the 8th Massachusetts Infantry, under the command of Col. Benjamin F. Butler, reached Annapolis on his march to Washington in April of 1861. Butler was quickly followed by troops from New York, who set up camp in the Yard during the Civil War.

HISTORIC MARKER
About twenty yards from the Butler marker is a small
plaque, on the wall of Luce Hall, marking the location
where the Peggy Stewart, an eighteenth-century brig,
was burned and sunk along with its cargo during the
Annapolis Tea Party just prior to the Revolutionary War.
The timbers of the ship were discovered during excava-
tion work for the construction of a new sea wall,
circa 1900.

Glen Warner Soccer Facility, aerial view. *Courtesy CSD Architects*

A. Anders, USAF (Ret.), Class of 1955, a former astronaut
and CEO of General Dynamics.

Architecturally, the Warner facility was designed to
complement and be a good neighbor to the towering
Bancroft Hall. With its modest size, grayish-buff color,
and flat roof, it does not obstruct the water view from
Bancroft Hall, but its dome creates a special entrance to
the stadium.[38]

Round the corner to the front of Luce Hall to see
one of the most unusual (and unexpected) memorials
in the Yard.

THE JAPANESE PAGODA

In front of Luce Hall is a tall pagoda, which was built in
memory of Japanese ambassador Hiroshi Saito, who died
in Washington, D.C., in 1939. By order of President
Franklin Roosevelt, his remains were sent home on a
U.S. Navy ship, USS *Astoria*.

With thirteen tiers of soft granite and the four
Buddhas represented in Sanskrit characters at the base, the
Japanese Pagoda is designed in the style of the Fujiwara
period of the eighth or ninth century. It was presented to
the Naval Academy in 1940. Hiroshi's widow and children were so grateful they determined to erect a memorial to him to commemorate his life and dedication to
Japanese–American relations. During World War II, the
monument was highly criticized, but it was never moved.

The trio of buildings in front of you is, from left
to right, Luce Hall, Macdonough Hall, and the Scott
Natatorium.

The Japanese Pagoda.
*Courtesy Special
Collections & Archives
Division, Nimitz
Library, U.S. Naval
Academy*

LUCE HALL ●

Luce Hall was built in 1919 to house the Department of Seamanship and Navigation, as indicated on the etched façade. It was named for Rear Adm. Stephen B. Luce, Class of 1847, a prominent seamanship instructor and a founder of the Naval War College in Newport, Rhode Island. At the center of Luce Hall is a bust of Vice Adm. John D. Bulkeley, Class of 1933, who received the Medal of Honor in World War II for evacuating Gen. Douglas MacArthur and his family from the Philippines. There are two steel torpedoes flanking the back entrance of the building.

MACDONOUGH HALL ●

Macdonough Hall is the oldest of this trio and was designed by Flagg to match Dahlgren Hall in its exterior style. Originally designed to be a boathouse and house the Department of Seamanship, it was actually built to house a gymnasium and classroom for seamanship. It was named for Capt. Thomas Macdonough, who served under Preble and with Decatur in the Tripolitan Wars and was responsible for a strategic victory on Lake Champlain against the British in 1814. It is now used as an athletic facility and the site of famous Brigade boxing matches, including the famous one between Lt. Col. Oliver North and former Secretary of the Navy and renowned author James Webb, both Class of 1968.

Macdonough Hall, circa 1916, before Dewey Field was dredged. *Courtesy Special Collections & Archives Division, Nimitz Library, U.S. Naval Academy*

MACDONOUGH'S CANNON
To the right of Macdonough Hall is a large 24-pound cannon. It was captured by Commodore Macdonough during the Battle of Lake Champlain. The muzzle has a dent from an American shot, which caused the gun to recoil and fire, resulting in the death of the British commander Downie.

SCOTT NATATORIUM ⬤

Macdonough Hall is connected to the Scott Natatorium, named for Rear Adm. Norman Scott, Class of 1911. As a midshipman, Rear Adm. Scott was instrumental in introducing competitive swimming to the Naval Academy. He later earned a Medal of Honor during the Battle of Savo Island in World War II.

Before the Olympic-sized pool was built in Lejeune Hall, the Natatorium was the site of the largest "swimming tank" in the Yard (and, arguably, one of the largest indoor tile pools in the United States at one time). It is 150 feet long, 60 feet wide, and 10 feet deep; it was fed water from artesian wells, filtered through sand and then passed through a violet-ray machine. At the time, this "advanced" purification system occupied most of the building's basement.[39]

For generations of midshipmen, Scott Natatorium was where they were required to pass the first-class swim test. (This test is now usually held in the Olympic-sized pool at Lejeune Hall.) Before graduation, every midshipman had to successfully complete the "burning ship exercise" by jumping off a ten-meter platform that was lowered from the ceiling above the pool. For some midshipmen, it was daunting. "We had this extension ladder that you would crank down from the ceiling, so you were in the center of the pool with no structure around you," as described by Chris Kidd, Class of 1976. "It was akin to standing on the top of a phone pole with nothing around you." Kidd was a strong swimmer, so he was part of a squad of midshipmen who gave his peers swimming lessons. He also coached them off the platform, but he couldn't push them. They had to do it on their own. "You essentially climbed up what was an aluminum extension ladder up into the rafters and you stood on this platform and you looked down and you had to step off." Scott Natatorium holds many memories for the more acrophobic midshipmen.

The pool of the Scott Natatorium in the 1920s. *Courtesy Special Collections & Archives Division, Nimitz Library, U.S.*

If you turn around and put your back to Macdonough's cannon, you can see Ingram Field across the parking lot in front of you, with Rickover Hall on the far side of Ingram, and Michelson and Chauvenet halls lining the left perimeter of Ingram. Ingram Field is named for Adm. Jonas H. Ingram, Class of 1907, Medal of Honor recipient, and Director of Athletics at the Academy in 1925–30. Walk around the left side of Ingram Field and up the steps to Radford Terrace, the plaza between the Michelson and Chauvenet Halls, one of the places where the second-class midshipmen (juniors) hold their Ring Dance every May. The terrace is named for Adm. Arthur W. Radford, Class of 1916, Chairman of the Joint Chiefs of Staff, 1953–57.

Michelson, Chauvenet, and Rickover halls are three of the four buildings designed by John Carl Warnecke (Nimitz Library is behind Michelson). Built in the 1960s and 1970s, this group of buildings changed the landscape of the Yard as much as Ernest Flagg's creations did.

JOHN CARL WARNECKE
AND THE MOREELL COMMISSION

By the middle of the twentieth century, the Academy
was once again outgrowing its facilities. While Flagg had
intended to provide a somewhat elastic plan that could be
expanded, his academic facilities became sorely outdated
and were too small. A special commission headed by
Adm. Ben Moreell was appointed in 1961 to produce a
new plan for the Academy—the first major construction
program in more than fifty years. Moreell is known as the
"Father of the Seabees," and a monument outlining his
contributions to the Navy stands in front of the
Levy Center.

The report the commission submitted in January 1962
included a bold proposal to annex three city blocks of historic Annapolis outside Gate Three (the Maryland Avenue
gate) between Hanover and King George streets. The
report's authors claimed that only two historic buildings
would be affected and that these two homes could easily
be relocated. "There is no satisfactory alternate location for
such a building that will provide for future growth, have
adequate size, reasonable accessibility, and provide a good
building site at a reasonable cost."[40]

A copy of the plan was leaked to the *Baltimore Sun*
before the plan had been properly vetted with city officials. The city was incensed that they were not consulted
prior to the completion of the study and protested that the
three blocks were vital to preserving the history and char-
acter of Annapolis, one of the few American cities with
visible remnants of early American culture. "The three
blocks of Annapolis the Naval Academy seeks to acquire
are an integral part of the old city. They first appear on the
map prepared by James Stoddert, the surveyor, in 1718.
Over the years the inhabitants of these blocks have played
a part in the history of Maryland and its capital city."[41]

This report, prepared by the local preservationists, outlined more than a half-dozen historic homes and locations located within these 9.6 acres, including the Peggy Stewart House, where the Stewart family watched colonists burn Mr. Stewart's brig, *Peggy Stewart*, to protest British taxes.

The dispute was also waged in the *Baltimore Sun*:

> "We are gravely concerned with the implications behind the proposed expansion of the Naval Academy into portions of historic Annapolis," Robert J. Kerr, executive director of Historic Annapolis, Inc., said yesterday. . . . "Mr. Kerr said that neither he nor the city's Planning and Zoning Commission had been told of the plan and that its announcement yesterday caught the town 'completely off guard.'"[42]

And so the original plan was scuttled.

A new proposal was developed that suggested the use of tennis courts that ran along Stribling Walk, as well as Dewey Basin (if it were filled in to create more land). A competitive bid landed John Carl Warnecke and Associates the contract to design a master plan that included a new science and engineering building. Warnecke was a close friend of First Lady Jackie Kennedy and had also been hired to create contemporary buildings to complement the historic structures at Lafayette Square, directly across the street from the White House. He had also built libraries at numerous other universities, including Stanford, so his qualifications fit the Academy's needs.

There was concern that the new math and science building would block the view of the Severn from the Chapel, destroying the relationship the center of the Yard had with the water. A compromise was described in the June 1965 issue of *Architectural Record*: "[B]y dividing the building into two parts, separated by a plaza, some of the traditional sense of continuity to the water will be retained."[43] It also created *two* naming opportunities: one to be named for Professor William Chauvenet, the first Naval Academy math professor, and one for Dr. Albert Michelson, Nobel Prize–winning scientist.

While Warnecke's plans for Chauvenet and Michelson Halls included building on tennis courts, his designs for the new library and the new engineering building (Nimitz and Rickover halls)—plus the later addition of the Brigade Activities Center (Alumni Hall)—called for the destruction of three historic buildings in the Yard: Isherwood, Melville, and Griffin. These buildings had been named for, respectively: Benjamin F. Isherwood, the first chief of the Bureau of Steam Engineering; George Wallace Melville, the leading survivor of the doomed 1879 Arctic Expedition on the *Jeannette*; and Rear Adm. Robert S. Griffin, former engineer-in-chief of the Navy (1913–21). There just was not enough space for all of the buildings to coexist.

Warnecke took great care to reflect the Beaux-Arts style of the Flagg design in style and proportions, by creating mansard-style roofs and façades with distinct horizontal layers. The Warnecke additions and Alumni Hall were signs of progress and growth for the Academy and were necessary to educate and train 21st-century naval leaders, but they signaled the biggest physical and structural change to the Yard since Flagg put his stamp on the place at the turn of the twentieth century.

MICHELSON AND CHAUVENET HALLS ⬤

Named for Nobel Prize–winning scientist Dr. Albert A. Michelson and original Naval Academy faculty member William Chauvenet, these twin structures are somewhat reminiscent of the Beaux-Arts style so embraced by

The steps leading up to Radford Terrace, the plaza between Michelson and Chauvenet. *Courtesy Jamie Howren Photography*

Ernest Flagg: copper, mansard-style roofs and symmetry. However, the buildings are intended to serve as think tanks for the study of science and mathematics.

The first American to receive a Nobel Prize in physics, Dr. Michelson successfully measured the velocity of light while serving as a physics professor at the Naval Academy between 1877 and 1879. He conducted the experiment that led to his groundbreaking discovery here in the Yard. As a reminder of the genius that was generated on these shores, a memorial dedicated to Dr. Michelson's experiment is commemorated on Radford Terrace, between Michelson and Chauvenet. (This was the shoreline of the Severn River at the time of his experiment.) Two identical bronze plaques describing the experiment are placed at either end of the path. You can follow the approximate path of Professor Michelson's groundbreaking experiment to measure the velocity of

The old and new: Michelson on the left, Chauvenet to the right, with the Mexican Monument directly in the center, providing a symbolic directional arrow straight to the Severn River.
Courtesy Jamie Howren Photography

light by walking along this series of eighty circular stainless-steel plates spaced eighteen inches apart. Dr. Michelson immortalized the Yard and the Naval Academy as a place for exceptional academic achievement— not just as a training ground for seafaring warriors.

The William Chauvenet took charge of the Philadelphia Naval Asylum School in 1842 with the support of George Bancroft. Chauvenet, the son of a French veteran who emigrated to America at the fall of the First Empire, graduated from Yale with high honors in 1840. The twenty-three-year-old Chauvenet

The stainless-steel plates on Radford Terrace.
Courtesy Jamie Howren Photography

Contemporary in architectural design but vaguely reminiscent of Flagg's Beaux-Arts style, Michelson Hall houses science laboratories and classrooms. *Courtesy Jamie Howren*

accepted an appointment as professor of mathematics in 1841.

To the north of Chauvenet and Michelson along the waterfront are Rickover Hall and Nimitz Library. They are connected by a raised terrace named for Chief

---

DID YOU KNOW?

Albert Michelson, a Polish immigrant, was almost denied admission to the Academy. While he earned an appointment to the Academy through then-President Ulysses S. Grant, the allotted quota had been filled. Through a personal interview with President Grant, an additional "at-large" position was created for Michelson and he was allowed to enter as a member of the Class of 1873. He was one of twenty-nine midshipmen to graduate that year. Michelson's collection of private papers is stored in the Nimitz Library. A virtual tour of this collection can be viewed at www.usna.edu/LibExhibits/Michelson/Michelson_personal.html#.

Engineer Isherwood.
Exposed to the elements,
this sun-drenched, concrete
plaza can be scorchingly hot
in the summer and bitterly
windswept in the winter.
Continue down the walk-
way on the water side of
Michelson and then climb
the stairs to Isherwood
Terrace.

Professor William Chauvenet.
*Courtesy Special Collections
& Archives Division, Nimitz
Library, U.S. Naval Academy*

NIMITZ LIBRARY ⊖
Completed in the spring
of 1973 and also designed by Warnecke, Nimitz Library
(straight ahead) is a modern library facility with more
than 150,000 square feet of space. In 1845, the original
Naval Academy library was comprised of only 361 books
in its collection. Today,
however, the Nimitz
Library houses an exten-
sive collection of more
than 365,000 volumes,
as well as artwork, maps,
and documents, includ-
ing Audubon bird prints,
Ansel Adams photographs,
and a letter written by
George Washington to
John Paul Jones in 1787.

Bronze bust of Adm. Chester
Nimitz. *Courtesy Jamie Howren
Photography*

In the lobby is a
heroic-sized bust of Fleet
Adm. Chester Nimitz,
Class of 1905 and the
commander of more than

Nimitz Library. *Courtesy U.S. Naval Academy Photographic Services*

six hundred Allied ships in the Pacific campaign of World War II. Admiral Nimitz sat for the clay model of this bust in 1948. The sculptor, Felix W. de Weldon, supervised the casting of this bronze copy, which was unveiled and dedicated in conjunction with the dedication of the Library in 1973. de Weldon also sculpted the Marine Corps (Iwo Jima) Memorial in Arlington, Virginia.

Also on the first floor of the Library is a thin glass monument that resembles an ice sculpture. It commemorates those crewmembers of the USS *Thresher* and USS *Scorpion* who died when these two submarines were lost at sea on 10 April 1963 and 5 June 1968, respectively. Etched in the artwork are a submarine, Naval Academy and class crests, and many sea images. The artist, Eric S. Krag, is the son of a *Thresher* crewmember who perished aboard, Lt. Cdr. Robert Lee Krag, Class of 1950.

As the main library in the Yard, with a sizeable Special Collections and Archives department, the Nimitz Library's Naval Academy Archives is an affiliate of the National Archives and contains 400 manuscript collections, 35,000 bound volumes, and the official records

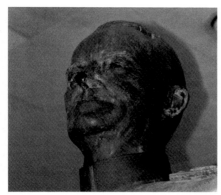

The nose of the Nimitz bronze is highly polished, probably from midshipmen rubbing it for good luck (like Admiral Rickover's bust in Rickover Hall). *Courtesy Jamie Howren Photography*

(RG 405) of the Naval Academy. When the naval lyceums in Brooklyn and Boston closed in 1888 and 1921, respectively, the Naval Academy inherited their collections as well.

Some notable items in the Nimitz Library's Special Collections include:

- Lt. Cdr. Harry F. Guggenheim Collection, approximately 2,900 volumes of literature, literary first editions, poetry, and aeronautics;
- Park Benjamin Collection, almost 1,200 volumes of early works on electricity and magnetism, including some by Descartes, Franklin, Galileo, and Ramelli;
- Benjamin West's copy of *Paradise Lost;*
- Edward J. Steichen Photography Collection, approximately 30,000 photographs and 580 books, including photographs by Steichen, Dorothea Lange, Edward Weston, and Margaret Bourke-White; established by Thomas J. Maloney, Class of 1927, on the occasion of Steichen's 90th birthday.

DID YOU KNOW?
The oldest book in the Nimitz collection is a 1487 Bible.

It is unusual for an undergraduate institution—especially one that does not support graduate research—to have such rich and publicly accessible collections. For a complete list of the special collections, go to: www.usna.edu/ Library/spec_coll.htm. They are accessible to researchers upon request.

RICKOVER HALL ⊖

Completed in 1975 and also designed by Warnecke, Rickover Hall (on the Severn River side of Nimitz Library) is named for Adm. Hyman G. Rickover, the father of the nuclear Navy and a member of the Class of 1922. It houses the Academy's engineering department and includes various labs and model engines designed to give the students simulated training for their future on ships, submarines, and in airplanes.

Rickover Hall contains a steam propulsion plant, a jet engine, five wind tunnels (both supersonic and subsonic),

Rickover Hall houses the largest college "tow tank" facility of its kind. Photo © 2006, Roger Miller. *Courtesy Roger Miller Photography*

and, in the basement, two tow tanks used to test ship
models in different sea states, which are simulated by the
wave maker at one end of a tank. One tow tank is 120
feet long, but the larger one is 380 feet long, 16 feet deep,
26 feet wide, and holds 1.25 million gallons of fresh water
(but the data collected can be corrected for the density of
salt water). Damage due to Hurricane Isabel in September
2003 was the worst to hit the Yard and Annapolis since
the 1600s and it took nearly two years to fully repair
the building. In the lobby of Rickover Hall is a bust of
Admiral Rickover and numerous large-scale ship models,
plus a sample gas turbine engine.

Continue down the stairs to the left of Nimitz Library
and curve around to the right to reach Alumni Hall.

In 2003, damage from Hurricane Isabel was widespread
throughout the Yard. *Courtesy U.S. Naval Academy
Photographic Services*

DID YOU KNOW?
Rickover Hall is one of three buildings in the Yard named for individuals who were living at the time of its completion. Hubbard Hall was named for Rear Adm. John Hubbard, and Wesley Brown Field House, which broke ground in 2006, is named for Lt. Cdr. Wesley A. Brown, Class of 1949, the first African American to graduate from the Naval Academy. A 140,000-square-foot facility, the Brown Field House will be located between the seventh wing of Bancroft Hall and the Santee Basin. It will house physical, medical, and combat-readiness training, and is scheduled to be completed in 2007.

Portrait of Adm. Hyman G. Rickover, Class of 1922. *Courtesy Special Collections & Archives Division, Nimitz Library, U.S. Naval Academy*

Admiral Rickover's initials inscribed in a metal beam and encased in Rickover Hall, made by the Admiral himself during ceremonies at the Naval Academy on 29 March 1974. *Courtesy Jamie Howren Photography*

DID YOU KNOW?
A chapter of Tau Beta Pi, the honorary engineering society, was established at the Naval Academy in 1984. A marker recognizing this admission stands next to the entrance of Rickover Hall.

ALUMNI HALL ⬤

Originally called the Brigade Activities Center, this building is one of a few facilities in the Yard that can seat the entire brigade at once. It holds more than 6,000 seats and is used for sporting events, lectures, and concerts.[44] Since it was funded primarily by Naval Academy alumni, it was officially named Alumni Hall. (Many of the newer buildings in the Yard are partially or completely funded through private sources.)

Each of the building's three entrances is adorned with a bronze Naval Academy coat of arms, donated by the Class of 1947, and filled with metallic mementos: class rings, uniform buttons, medals and decorations, and uniform insignia. These items were thrown into a vat of melted bronze before it was poured into the mold.[45] Three buildings—Melville Hall, Griffin Hall, and Isherwood Hall—were demolished to make room in the Yard for Alumni Hall and the three entrances are named after the three buildings Alumni Hall replaced (the fourth entrance is simply called the East Entrance).

On the walls of the main lobby of Alumni Hall is a group of oil paintings by Tom Freeman, a well-known

Alumni Hall. *Courtesy U.S. Naval Academy Photographic Services*

The entire Brigade of Midshipmen seated in Alumni Hall.
Courtesy U.S. Naval Academy Photographic Services

naval artist whose works also hang at the USS *Arizona* Memorial in Pearl Harbor, Hawaii, and in the presidential wing of the White House. The paintings were donated by the Class of 1961 and depict events in which members of the class participated: (from left to right) *Action at Hue, Vietnam; Carrier Group at Sea: USS* Ranger *(CV-61), USS* Eversole *(DD-789) and USS* Truxton *(CGN-35); and Rescue at Sea of a Downed B52 Crew Off Guam by USS* Barb *(SSN-596).*

Just inside the Isherwood entrance (at the top of the stairs) is a colorfully painted wooden sternboard from USS *Franklin.* (Compare it to the sternboard from the USS *Macedonian* hanging just inside the entrance of Dahlgren Hall.)

WORDEN FIELD

To your left, as you read on the monument that lists
the names of graduates who sacrificed their lives in the
Vietnam War, is a large, open field with homes dotting
two sides. This is Worden Field, the Yard's official parade
grounds. The Brigade of Midshipmen has been holding formal parades here since the early 1900s. Named for
Rear Adm. John L. Worden, a former superintendent and
the commanding officer of the USS *Monitor,* one of the
ironclad ships involved in the historic Civil War battle, the
USS *Monitor* versus the CSS *Virginia* (formerly the USS
Merrimack), the field is rich in military tradition and replete
with patriotic pomp. Rear Adm. Worden's presentation
sword is on exhibition in the Naval Academy Museum.

Above: Brigade of Midshipmen on Worden Field. *Courtesy U.S. Naval Academy Photographic Services*

Right: Rear Adm. John Worden, mid-1800s. *Courtesy Special Collections & Archives Division, Nimitz Library, U.S. Naval Academy*

THE PARADE FIELD HOMES

In 1867, ten acres of land along College Creek were purchased from St. John's College (the neighboring liberal arts college, just across Maryland Avenue from the Academy). In 1871, four more acres were purchased and, in 1891, twelve additional acres, completing a long-term land acquisition plan. Part of this new property was designated for Academy housing. Washington, D.C., architect George O. Von Nerta was hired to build residences in the area outlining Worden Field. The red-brick Victorian Queen Anne Revival duplexes, on Upshur and Rodgers

roads, feature wraparound porches, formal foyers, tall
ceilings, and fireplaces with hand-carved oak and cherry
mantels.[46]

HUBBARD HALL ●

Walk away from Alumni Hall down Decatur Road to Hill
Bridge. As you cross this bridge, you will notice a crew
house off to your left and you might also be lucky enough
to see the swan-like sculls gliding up and down College
Creek. This building is Hubbard Hall, built in 1931, and
named for a former Naval Academy crew team member,
Rear Adm. John Hubbard, Class of 1870 (the first building
in the Yard to be named for a living person). The crew
team has a storied history here in the Yard, having earned
two Olympic gold medals—in the 1920 games at Antwerp
and in the 1952 games at Helsinki. Crew is one of the
oldest team sports practiced at the Academy.

Just beyond Hubbard Hall is Bishop Stadium, the
Academy's baseball facility, named for Max F. Bishop,
the Academy's baseball coach 1938–62. The stadium
clubhouse is named for Ambassador William H. G.
Fitzgerald, Class of 1931, and the field is named
Terwilliger Brothers Field for Jackson, Class of 1963,
Bruce, Class of 1964, and George, Class of 1969, all of
whom played Navy baseball.

THE OBSERVATORY ●

Just across the street from Hubbard Hall is an observatory
that houses the Naval Academy's original telescope.
Built in 1991 as a gift of the Class of 1941, it is in active
use by students and professors studying astronomy. Farther
along Bowyer Road (and in front of Halligan Hall) is
Lawrence Field, named for Capt. James Lawrence, hero
of the War of 1812, and famous for his dying words that
shout from the flag hanging in Memorial Hall: "Don't
give up the ship!"

Up the hill and behind the Observatory sits a section of family housing called the Perry Circle housing area, but nicknamed the "bungalows." Constructed elsewhere, the first fifteen of these houses were first shipped to the Yard by train in 1919 and assembled in their current location. These structures were originally meant to be temporary structures, alleviating a housing shortage for faculty and staff.

HALLIGAN HALL ●

Off in the distance, down Bowyer Road, is a red-tiled building designed by Henry Ives Cobb, built in 1903 as a Marine barracks. Born in Brookline, Massachusetts, Cobb studied at Harvard and MIT and made his reputation as the architect for several buildings at the University of Chicago. Like Flagg, he was trained in the École de Beaux-Arts in Paris. The Bower Road building became the first location for the Naval Postgraduate School (now located in Monterey, California) in 1919 and named in 1937 for the school's first director, Rear Adm. John Halligan, Jr., Class of 1898.[47] Today, the building houses Academy support staff.

At the end of the bridge, take a right, cross the street, and head up the hill on Phythian Road. This high ground was the site of a colonial house built for the Sprigg family, a dinner host to President George Washington during Washington's 1773 trip to Annapolis to attend the theater.

THE NAVAL ACADEMY CEMETERY★

Sited between the Severn River and its estuary College Creek, this picturesque piece of land was purchased by the U.S. government in 1868 as part of a two-parcel

★ As a courtesy, please stay on the paved roads and avoid walking on the grass. For more information and to look up specific individuals, go to www.usna.edu/cemetery.

purchase of more than one hundred acres, the largest addition ever to the Naval Academy. Here is where the Naval Academy chose to lay out a cemetery for graduates, one of only a handful of college campuses (including the U.S. Military Academy at West Point) that maintain an active cemetery. This is also the site of several former Naval Academy hospitals, the most recent one designed by Ernest Flagg in 1906. This building on the hill can be seen from the Severn River and is still used as a medical facility, providing health services to the Brigade of Midshipmen, as well as Academy staff and families living and working in the Annapolis area.

Its small size and notable residents make the Naval Academy Cemetery one of the most unique and important cemeteries in the country. Of course, for the families who have buried loved ones there, it's also personal. For the Mustin clan, an extended Navy family with five genera-

The Naval Academy Cemetery, with a western view of Forrest Sherman Field, the Severn River, and the Severn River Bridge. *Courtesy Jamie Howren Photography*

tions of Academy graduates and many friends buried in this cemetery, it is full of memories. Vice Adm. Hank Mustin, Class of 1955, and his wife, Lucy, feel connected to the spot, "We go every Christmas and put flowers on my parents' graves. There, the funerals are more intimate. You know everyone and it's small. . . . You walk around and feel like you're among friends."

The natural vegetation that shelters—and almost hides—this quiet oasis includes oaks, mountain laurel, rhododendron, English boxwood and azalea, dogwood, flowering cherries and hydrangea, forsythia, and spirea.

Halfway up the historic "Strawberry Hill," you'll notice a pink granite headstone right next to the sidewalk. This is the first of two graves of former superintendents for whom bridges are named, bridges within view of their respective tombs. Harry Hill's headstone overlooks Hill Bridge, the bridge you crossed to access the cemetery. And at the conclusion of your tour, you will notice the grave of Aubrey Fitch, which overlooks Fitch Foot Bridge.

Close to the road is a large, polished granite headstone emblazoned with the surname Kristensen. One of the first casualties of the global war on terrorism to be buried here, Lt. Cdr. Erik Kristensen, Class of 1995, was a Navy SEAL

The Celtic cross, here surrounded by mature oak trees, is a common sight in many cemeteries. It combines a cross intersecting a ring, representing eternity. *Courtesy Jamie Howren Photography*

killed in Afghanistan in June 2005. His epitaph quotes
Herman Melville: "Quelled on the wing like eagles struck
in air—forever they slumber young and fair." Vice Adm.
James Stockdale, Class of 1946, Medal of Honor recipient,
former Vietnam POW, and once candidate for vice president, who died in July 2005, was buried with full honors
here as well.

The Fuller family headstones. *Courtesy Jamie Howren Photography*

Wind around to the right onto Cushing Road and
look slightly to the left and you'll see three Fuller family
member graves. Serving as Marine Corps Commandant
from 1930 to 1934, Maj. Gen. Ben Hebard Fuller was a
member of the Class of 1889. Fuller died in 1937 and is
buried next to his son, Capt. Edward C. Fuller, of the
6th Marines, who was killed at the Battle of Belleau Wood
in World War I. Mrs. Katherine Heaton Offley Fuller,
wife of Gen. Ben Fuller and mother of Edward, rests
beside them.

Opposite the Fuller family plot, facing the Severn, is
a tall headstone with a large cross (a single cross one row

behind three graves of crosses). This is the final resting place of Charles Zimmerman, the legendary bandmaster at the Naval Academy who composed "Anchors Aweigh," and for whom the bandstand is named. Legend has it that he somehow fell out of the choir loft in the Naval Academy Chapel and later died of his injuries.

Farther up Cushing Road, off to the left is a tombstone of polished, black granite—flanked by columns. Here is buried Adm. Elmo Zumwalt, Chief of Naval Operations during the Vietnam War. He was responsible for directing the use of the defoliant Agent Orange and penned an autobiography about the controversy surrounding its use and the long-term health effects of the defoliant on his own son, who had served inVietnam during its use.

Behind you in the near distance is a large building that overlooks the cemetery. Originally built in 1958 as the newest wing of the former Naval Academy Hospital, Beach Hall now houses the U.S. Naval Institute and the Naval Academy Foundation. Its namesakes, Capt. Edward Latimer Beach Sr., Class of 1888, and Capt. Edward Beach Jr., Class of 1939, were both Academy graduates, both Navy captains, and both prolific authors. The younger Captain Beach circumnavigated the globe as commander of the nuclear-powered submarine USS *Triton* and wrote *Run Silent, Run Deep*. At the base of the small valley, directly below Beach Hall, you will see the younger Captain Beach's grave.

Behind Beach Hall is a medical clinic that overlooks the Severn, providing health services to the Brigade of Midshipmen, as well as the Academy's active duty staff and their families. The building in which it is housed was built in 1906 and was a full-service hospital until 1979.

At the fork in the road, bear right onto Sigsbee Way. Almost ninety degrees to the right is a grave with a column wrapped in oak and acanthus leaves. It is the grave

Beach Hall. *Courtesy U.S. Naval Academy Photographic Services*

of Lt. Cdr. Moreau Forrest, Class of 1862, who was the executive officer of the monitor *Kaekeuk* at Charleston, South Carolina, during the Civil War.

On one side of Forrest's grave, at the perimeter of the cemetery, is buried Adm. Husband Kimmel, Commander-in-Chief of the Pacific Fleet, when Pearl Harbor was attacked. Operating from the advanced base at Pearl Harbor, Kimmel led his fleet during the months of vigorous training that preceded the outbreak of the Pacific War. He was vilified after the attack for "dereliction of duty," fired from his command, and stripped of his rank. It took an act of Congress in 1999 to exonerate him.

On the other side of Forrest's grave lies a flat tombstone, that of John W. Philip, the commanding officer of the USS *Texas* during the Battle of Santiago in the Spanish-American War. You can see his swords in the Naval Academy Museum (in Preble Hall).

Turn around to your right and you'll see a series of Parker family graves. Commo. Foxhall Parker was the only superintendent to die in office. He was in office for one year and died in 1879. Parker's wife and family are buried next to him. While Foxhall had stayed with the Union during the Civil War, his older brother, Lt. William H. Parker, went south and became the superintendent of the Confederate Naval Academy, which was housed on the CSS *Patrick Henry,* a Confederate warship on the James River that doubled as a training vessel for Confederate midshipmen.

USS *Jeannette* memorial and Parker gravesite. *Courtesy Jamie Howren Photography*

Behind the Parker graves, you will notice the largest structure in the cemetery, a granite mound topped by an icicle-covered cross made of marble. It is a memorial (not a tomb) dedicated to the men who perished in the USS *Jeannette* Arctic Exploring Expedition of 1879–81. Lt. Cdr. George Washington DeLong, Class of 1865, led the *Jeannette* expedition from San Francisco up through the Bering Sea in hopes of learning about the movement of the ice cap. The crew was stranded on the ice for more than twenty-one months, eventually abandoning the *Jeannette*, dividing into two parties and attempting to escape in small boats and sleds. Many perished, including DeLong. Rescuers found his remains in a pile of rocks called a cairn, after which this monument is modeled. Designed by Academy professor Lt. George P. Colvocoresses, it was erected in 1890. DeLong's "ice journal," a small notebook in which he kept a running account of events, is preserved in the Naval Academy Museum.

Just off to the side of the *Jeannette* monument is a gravestone that memorializes those Americans killed in the Battle of Vera Cruz in Mexico in 1847. This is one of the oldest monuments in the cemetery and one of the few written in a foreign language.

Farther down the hill on the left is the grave of James Booth Lockwood, a West Point graduate and the only Army officer buried in this cemetery, who starved to death on the Greeley Expedition at Cape Sabine in 1884. His father was one of the seven original faculty members here at the Academy and James grew up in the Yard. Another Lockwood, Henry Hayes, who was also a West Point graduate and led a brigade at Gettysburg, is also buried here.

Keep walking toward the water along Sigsbee Way and you'll notice a clipped column, a Roman tradition symbolizing a life cut short. This has been erected in memory of Cdr. Edward Terry, former commandant of Midshipmen, whose verbose and poetic epitaph reads:

He served with distinction in the battle at New Orleans, Vicksburg, Port Hudson and Mobile,

and throughout his naval career was conspicuous
for his nautical skills, his professional attainments,
his remarkable coolness and courage, and for his
unswerving virtue and truth. His last cruise was
as Fleet Captain in the Pacific 1878–80, and upon
that Station he contracted the disease that led to
his death. He lived and died without fear and
without reproach.

Farther along on the left is a large obelisk, the memorial to Commo. Isaac Mayo, one of the few people born in
the eighteenth century to be commemorated here. Mayo
was a loyal Marylander and submitted a letter of resigna-
tion at the onset of the Civil War because he expected
Maryland to secede. When the state remained in the
Union, he tried unsuccessfully to withdraw his letter.
Despondent over his actions, he allegedly committed sui-
cide and his widow erected this stone on this site in 1870.
There is no record that his body was actually transferred
here from its original burial site.

Commander Cushing's burial site, late 1800s. *Courtesy Special
Collections & Archives Division, Nimitz Library, U.S. Naval
Academy*

Grave of Cdr. William Barker Cushing.
Courtesy Jamie Howren Photography

At the curve in the road, on the right, overlooking the Severn, is a trio of graves: Lt. Cdr. Charles W. Flusser, Cdr. William Barker Cushing, and Lt. Samuel Preston. Cushing was responsible for securing the burial sites for Flusser and Preston. Commander Cushing was a famous Union naval officer with a fearless reputation. His most noted action was exploding the confederate ironclad CSS *Albemarle* in retribution for the death of his good friend Flusser, killed in battle by the *Albemarle*. Cushing was determined to destroy the *Albemarle*. He steered a small boat at night just under the bow of the ironclad and rammed a spar torpedo into the ship, then jumped overboard and escaped to a nearby swamp. The ensign of the *Albemarle* is part of the Museum's extensive collection of flags. Among Cushing's other famous actions was in the Battle of Fort Fisher, one of the last major southern strongholds on the coast of North Carolina.

Cushing was assigned this most prominent cemetery location and given one of the most distinctive tombs because he was designated the most famous naval hero of the Civil War. Cushing was forced to resign from the

Academy for poor grades and bad conduct, but Flusser helped him to get a commission in the Navy. Cushing was eternally grateful for Flusser's assistance and ensured him a burial spot nearby. Preston was killed while serving next to Cushing at the Battle of Fort Fisher, so Cushing also wanted his buddy awarded a burial spot near him.

Infant headstones in the Academy Cemetery. *Courtesy Jamie Howren Photography*

This cemetery is also the final resting place of Theodore Gordon Ellyson, "the first naval aviator." As you head down the hill, look to the left for his headstone. Halfway down the hill, in the small valley on the left, is a section where many children and infants are buried. According to a handwritten ledger called the "Book of the Dead," most of them died as a result of premature birth. Many can be identified by a small lamb resting on top of these tombs. At the time, children of families stationed here at the Academy were eligible for burial here.

When you get to the point where the road evens out, look to the right for a flat tombstone with an anchor on top and the etched names of two midshipmen, William Edward Traylor Neumann and Thomas Ward Jr. Both were killed in a turret explosion aboard the USS *Missouri* in 1904. Neumann was engaged to Ward's sister at the time.

Farther down on the left, you will notice a series of small, thin markers that are weathered and moss-covered. A total of sixty of these gravestones identify the crew of the USS *Huron*, victims of a shipwreck off the coast of Cape Hatteras in 1877. The bodies were originally buried on the beach, but many were relocated here, even though the USS *Huron* and its crew had no connection to the Naval Academy.

DID YOU KNOW?
Nine headstones were moved to the Academy Cemetery after it was established in 1868. No one is certain if the bodies of the dead were also moved. The nine individuals are:

- *Two sailors from the USS* Preble, *the first Naval Academy training ship, who died in 1852;*
- *Commo. and Mrs. Henry Ballard, who died in 1855— probably on their nearby family plantation;*
- *Lt. Isaac Strain, who died in 1857 while exploring the Isthmus of Panama;*
- *Commo. Isaac Mayo, who died in 1861 at his home just outside Annapolis;*
- *Lt. Cdr. Charles Flusser, who was killed aboard the USS* Miami *in 1864;*
- *Lt. Samuel W. Preston, killed in action at Fort Fisher in 1865;*
- *Baby Arthur Farquhar, child of a commandant of Midshipmen.*

Turn your attention to the right to see the polished black marble grave of Adm. Arleigh Burke, former chief of naval operations and namesake for the Arleigh Burke–class guided-missile destroyer, an image of which is etched on the headstone. He was insistent his epitaph simply read: "Arleigh Burke, Sailor."

Mrs. Henry Ballard's headstone. *Courtesy Jamie Howren Photography*

DID YOU KNOW?
The highest ranking individual buried in the Cemetery is Fleet Adm. Ernest J. King. Among the lowest ranking individuals is Angus McInnis, a blacksmith for the Naval Academy, who died in 1898. Can you find his grave? It is a small marker located near the road along Sigsbee Way.

DID YOU KNOW?
Five chiefs of naval operations are buried in the Cemetery: Standley, King, Burke, McDonald, and Zumwalt. One commandant of the Marine Corps is buried here, Fuller. Nineteen superintendents are buried here, as well as eight Medal of Honor recipients

The only five-star admiral buried here is Fleet Adm. Ernest J. King, who served as the chief of naval operations throughout World War II. His grave is closest to McCandless Road, which is perpendicular to Cushing. If you walk inland, along McCandless Road, you'll see the trio of King family graves off to the left.

As you head down McCandless toward the Severn, take a right onto Ramsay Road and follow the curve of the road around to the right. As College Creek comes into view, look up the hill to your right for a few scattered graves overlooking the creek. Here's where you'll see the headstone of Adm. Aubrey W. Fitch, hero of the Battle of Coral Sea and former superintendent, which overlooks Fitch Bridge.

Only a few cemeteries in this country can boast such a large concentration of heroes and individuals who have dedicated their lives to the service of their country. The fact that many of them made a conscious decision to be buried here—where they attended college, rather than in a family or community plot—speaks volumes about the personal significance of their experience in this place called the Yard.

THE COLUMBARIUM

Just below the Cemetery, tucked in the nook created by the bottom of the hill, is the place where Academy graduates can be inurned. The Academy recognized that the Cemetery was running out of space for its burgeoning

A vintage view of the Cemetery, where the Columbarium is now located. *Courtesy Special Collections & Archives Division, Nimitz Library, U.S. Naval Academy*

alumni population, but that the ground left for expansion was below sea level and, therefore, unsuitable for burial. With seed money donated by the George Olmsted Foundation in memory of General Olmsted's brother, Ens. Jerauld Olmsted, Class of 1922, the Naval Academy Alumni Association raised a total of $500,000 in private donations to build the original Columbarium that was completed in 1987.

Designed with 160 feet of white marble facing, the Columbarium comfortably spreads out horizontally along College Creek and contains 2,088 niches. One of the first alumni to be inurned there was Lt. William Blake Ramsey, Class of 1983. He and his fiancée, Kristen Waller, were tragically killed in a car accident in the summer of 1987. He was the Color Company Commander, in charge of the "company" ranked first in the brigade. She was his "Color Girl." They are inurned together and, in their memories, their families annually present a sword to the Color

Company commander and a string of pearls to the woman selected to be the Color Girl.

Centered in the structure is also a memorial to all Academy alumni who have died in the line of duty but whose bodies were never recovered. A fundraising effort by the Class of 1959 is underway to significantly expand the Columbarium and to physically connect it with the Cemetery above.

CONCLUSION

Once you finish touring the Cemetery, head down the hill the back way and cross to the middle of the Fitch Foot Bridge. From there, you can catch a panoramic view of the Cemetery and the Columbarium on one side of College Creek, and the lineup of contemporary structures on the other, all surrounded by water. One campus with a memorable mixture of past and present.

Ernest Flagg created a "new Academy" that could serve as the leadership crucible for the world's preeminent Navy. But even he could not have fathomed the dynamic nature of the Naval Academy nor its growth. As new generations of men and women train and toil here, the advancing needs of the midshipmen *and* evolving technology will continue to dictate the additional facilities the Yard must provide. The space and the place will perpetually adapt. But, fortunately, the relics of previous wars and their wartime heroes will continue to offer up reminders of how we arrived. It is up to all of us—midshipmen, alumni, staff, historians, Congress, and taxpayers—to ensure the Naval Academy and the Yard do not lose the heritage. It's what protects its future.

PART III *All around the yard*

All around the yard

Over the years, many historically significant works of art have been donated to the Naval Academy in recognition of the Yard as a fitting place for housing and preserving American military antiques. Cannons and cannon shot, paintings, sculptures, books and prints, maps, china, and weapons are on display outside in park-like settings and inside the U.S. Naval Academy Museum, and as décor in building lobbies and foyers.

"SO PROUDLY WE HAIL"
More than six hundred historic flags grace the walls of buildings around the Yard. Some are housed and displayed in the Museum, others can be found in the lobby, corridors, and auditorium of Mahan Hall, and some are on display in Memorial and Smoke halls inside Bancroft Hall.

The most famous of the flags is the Perry flag. After Oliver Hazard Perry's victory over the British squadron on Lake Erie, he sent this flag and other pennants and ensigns to Washington. In 1849, President James K. Polk designated that these trophy flags be housed and maintained at the Academy as part of its permanent collection.

Celebrations planned for the centennial of the War of 1812 generated renewed interest in the flags. But time had not been kind to the collection, so Congress appropriated $30,000 to hire an expert on flag conservation to repair the Academy's collection and to construct proper exhibit cases.

Amelia Fowler, the flag conservator who later was hired to restore the Star Spangled Banner in 1914, and her team of forty seamstresses sewed over every square

Midshipmen pay respect to the Perry battle flag and Memorial Hall, 1925. *Courtesy Special Collections & Archives Division, Nimitz Library, U.S. Naval Academy*

inch of the 15,000 square yards of the Perry flag, as well as the other 171 flags. As H. C. Washburn described the process, "Mrs. Fowler's needlewomen, who averaged forty in number, began the arduous labor of sewing over by hand every square inch of the 15,000 square yards of 172 flags."[48] After restoration, the flags were placed in forty-one cases and twenty-three paneled spaces in Mahan and

---

DID YOU KNOW?
The value of an antique American flag is affected by (1) the star configuration, (2) the age, (3) the size, and (4) any specific history the flag might have.[49]

Smoke halls. The collection grew in the twentieth century with the addition of flags from World War I and II, as well as the conflicts in Korea and Vietnam.

All of the flags are available for examination and research with an appointment. Of note are:

- As you stand in Memorial Hall and face the Rotunda, you will notice two flags on either side of the main door. To the left is the flag flown on the battleship USS *South Dakota* during World War II, the same ship that is portrayed in the mural above the bronze doors in the Rotunda. To the right is a flag flown by the destroyer USS *Ozbourn* during the amphibious landing at Inchon during the Korean War.

- The ensign of the CSS *Albemarle* is a Confederate flag taken at the end of the Civil War when federal forces occupied Plymouth, North Carolina.

- A jack and pennant from the HMS *Guerriere,* captured by USS *Constitution* commanding officer Capt. Isaac Hull on 19 August 1812, is housed in the Museum.

- The ensign of the British frigate HMS *Macedonian,* captured by Capt. Stephen Decatur and his crew on the USS *United States,* is on display in Mahan Hall. The *Macedonian*'s figurehead stands at the foot of Stribling Walk, across Maryland Avenue from Mahan Hall.

- The first U.S. flag officially carried ashore in Japan is housed in the Museum. This thirty-one-star flag was used by Commo. Matthew C. Perry in his meeting with the Japanese commissioners at Uraga, Province of Sagami, near Yokohama, 14 July 1853.

- The jack from the USS *Arizona* was flown from its bow during the attack on Pearl Harbor, 7 December 1941.

- Ensign from the USS *Hornet* was flown during the launch of the Doolittle raid on Tokyo.
- A 26-star command pennant came from Commo. Jesse D. Elliott.
- The U.S. flags that were carried on Richard E. Byrd's first flight over the North Pole (1926) and his first flight over the South Pole (1929).

In 2005, the Perry flag was once again removed for conservation treatment at a cost of $50,000 (donated by the Class of 1954). This time, Deborah Trupin, a textile conservator from the New York State Office of Parks, Recreation and Historic Preservation, was hired to apply current textile conservation techniques to ensure the flag lasts another century (at least). Located at Peebles Island (near Albany), New York, Ms. Trupin and her team of professionals carefully removed all the cable stitching and linen background support of the Fowler treatment—more than 16,000 stitches and two layers of blue cotton fabric—to get down to the original flag. What was revealed was a brown fabric, now believed to be the original color, refuting the long-standing belief that the flag was blue.

KABOOM! VINTAGE ORDNANCE IN THE YARD

The Yard has long served as a repository for war relics, and the Naval Academy has been responsible for their preservation, exhibit, and use in educating future generations of Naval leaders and the public about our nation's rich naval heritage. Ernest Flagg had very specific ideas as to how they should be maintained: "The best possible treatment for them would be to provide wooden trucks such as they were originally mounted on. . . . These trucks would last, if kept painted, at least one hundred years, and the cost of the renewal would be trifling."[50]

Flagg's truck mounting recommendation was not implemented; many of the monuments were moved and placed on masonry platforms instead—most likely to augment his design of pedestrian walks that included intersections at strategic visual points or to complement architectural features of a nearby building.

The following is a list of guns, cannons, torpedoes, and shot displayed outside throughout the Yard as decorative elements to entryways, statues, and memorials (listed by general vicinity):

Administration Building and Chapel:
- Five-inch armored Spanish gun, captured from the Spanish armored cruiser *Vizcaya* during the Battle of Santiago Bay, Cuba, 1898, located at the corner of Maryland Avenue and Blake Road in front of the Administration Building;
- Spanish 18-pounder, named "San Cayentano," dated 1686, captured in the Mexican War, 1847, also located in front of the Administration Building
- Spanish 18-pounder, cast in Lima in 1769, captured in Mexican War, 1847, also located in front of the Administration Building;
- Turkish stone cannonball, the 600-pound type the Turks used during the conquest of Constantinople in 1453; gift of Ottoman Empire when Commo. John Rodgers visited in 1825 to negotiate the first treaty; located at the entryway to the Administration Building;
- Spanish 13-inch mortar, named "Seulilla," dated 1784, captured at Manila during the Spanish-American War, 1898, located on the Administration Building side of the Chapel;
- Spanish mortar, thirteen inches in diameter, captured in Manila during the Spanish-American War, 1898, located just outside St. Andrew's Chapel.

Bancroft Hall (and Tecumseh Court):

- Spanish 24-pounder named "El Menaleas," dated 1732, captured in the Mexican War, 1847, located on the masonry pedestal, upper steps, at the main entrance to Bancroft Hall;

- Spanish 24-pounder named "El Baiazeto," dated 1747, captured in the Mexican War, 1847, located on the masonry pedestal upper steps, at the main entrance of Bancroft Hall;

- French 24-pounder named "Le Gaillard," dated 1748, captured in the Mexican War, 1847, located on the masonry pedestal, lower steps, at the main entrance of Bancroft Hall;

- French 24-pounder named "Mars," dated 1755, captured in the Mexican War, 1847, located on the masonry pedestal, lower steps, at the main entrance of Bancroft Hall;

- French 24-pounder named "Le Mordicant," dated 1685, captured in the Mexican War, 1847, located on the masonry pedestal, outer entrance to Tecumseh Court (otherwise known as one of the "Virgin Cannons");

- French 24-pounder named "Le Grondeur," dated 1756, captured in the Mexican War, 1847, located on the masonry pedestal, outer entrance to Tecumseh Court (the other "Virgin Cannon");

- French 24-pounder named "Le Fier," dated 1755, captured in the Mexican War, 1847, located on the left side of the First Class Bench on Stribling Walk;

- Spanish 12-pounder named "San Albaro," dated 1673, captured in California during the Mexican War, 1847, located on the right side of the First Class Bench on Stribling Walk;

- French 24-pounder named "Le Robuste," dated 1755, captured in the Mexican War, 1847, located on the right side of the Second Class Bench on Stribling Walk;

- Spanish 12-pounder named "Jesus," dated 1675, captured in the Mexican War, 1847, located on the left side of the Second Class Bench on Stribling Walk.

Buchanan House:
- Five-inch armored Spanish gun captured from *Maria Teresa* during the Battle of Santiago Bay, Cuba, 1898, located in front of Buchanan House at the corner of Blake and Buchanan roads (see p. 35 for more information);
- Spanish 10-inch mortar, named "El Insolente," dated 1769, captured at Manila during the Spanish–American War, 1898, located on the Buchanan House side of the Chapel;
- Spanish 6-pounder, cast in Cuba in 1767, captured in the Mexican War, 1847, located in front of Buchanan House;
- Another Spanish 6-pounder, named "El Dromedario," dated 1766, captured in the Mexican War, 1847, also located in front of Buchanan House.

Dahlgren Hall:
- Dahlgren 30-pounder, rifled gun located at the landward end of Dahlgren Hall;
- Two Spanish one-pounder, rapid-fire Hotchkiss guns collected at Santiago Bay, Cuba, 1898, located at the landward end of Dahlgren Hall;
- German 75-mm howitzer captured at St. Raphael during the invasion of southern France, 1944, by forces from the U.S. Eighth Fleet, located at the landward end of Dahlgren Hall;
- Japanese type 91 aerial torpedo, gift of Rear Adm. W. R. Furlong, located at the landward end of Dahlgren Hall;

- Japanese type 93 torpedo, gift of Capt. R. M. Fortson, located at the landward end of Dahlgren Hall;
- Spanish 12-pounder, named "San Telesforo," dated 1793, captured in the Mexican War, 1847, located in front of landward end of Dahlgren Hall;
- Spanish 6-pounder, named "El Lefon," dated 1767, captured in Mexican War, 1847, located in front of landward end of Ward Hall;
- U.S. 15-inch battleship shells, located at landward end of Dahlgren Hall.

Gate 1:
- Twelve-pounder, 10-foot-long gun from USS *Oregon* designed by John Ericsson and the forerunner of the modern naval gun, located along the wall inside Gate One. Made of Yorkshire iron and reinforced with wrought-iron hoops, it was brought by Ericsson himself when he emigrated from England. It was shipped from the Philadelphia Navy Yard to the Naval Academy in 1867. (Its sister gun was the "Peacemaker," which exploded during a demonstration aboard the USS *Princeton* in the Potomac River in 1844, killing the secretary of state, the secretary of the navy, a U.S. senator, and a Navy bureau chief.)

Luce Hall:
- U.S. 15-inch battleship shells, located at the seaward entrance to Luce Hall.

Macdonough Hall:
- British 24-pounder captured by Capt. Thomas Macdonough from HMS *Confiance* during the Battle of Lake Champlain, 1814, located at the landward end of Macdonough Hall (see p. 131 for more information).

Mahan Hall:
- Dahlgren 30-pounder, rifled gun used aboard the USS *Oneida* during fighting in Pensacola, Florida, in the Civil War, located in front of Mahan Hall;
- Spanish 12-pounder named "San Leon," dated 1686, captured in the Mexican War, 1847, located in front of Mahan Hall;
- Spanish 17-inch mortar named "Cobres," dated 1779, captured at Manila during Spanish-American War, 1898, with 15-inch Dahlgren solid shot in its muzzle, located in front of Mahan Hall.

Mexican War Monument:
- Four Spanish 12-pounders, all captured in the California campaign of the Mexican War, 1847: "El Neptuno"—dated 1781, "El Faetonte"—dated 1781, "San Damien"—dated 1686, and "San Joseph"—dated 1687.

Preble Hall (U.S. Naval Academy Museum):
- British 4-pounder, recovered from the wreck of HMS *Augusta,* scuttled in the Delaware River, 1777, located in front of the Museum (see p. 37 for more information);
- Spanish breechloading, 8-pounder, reputedly made in the fifteenth century, captured in Alvarado, Mexico, 1847, located in the Museum;
- Two carronades from HMS *Cyane* captured by USS *Constitution* in the War of 1812, located in front of the Museum.

Sea Wall:
- U.S. Mark XIV torpedo, World War II, located in the Submarine Memorial near the Triton Light along the Sea Wall.

Visitor Center:
- 25-mm Swedish machine gun, gift of Swedish Navy in 1950, located at the Visitor Center.

BUSTS OR BUST!
NOTEWORTHY BUSTS AROUND THE YARD
By definition, a bust is a sculpture of a person that shows only the upper half of the body and it can include the head, shoulders, and chest of its subject. A "heroic bust" is one that is larger than life size.

It is interesting to note that, while there are numerous busts of noteworthy naval figures, there are no statues in outdoor, exposed spaces in the Yard—except for the life-size statue of Maj. Gen. John A. Lejeune, Class of 1888, just in front of the building named after him. In addition, there is a statue of Commo. George H. Perkins on the covered terrace outside Memorial Hall, sculpted by Daniel Chester French and signed by him in 1911. (This is actually a copy of the original, which was commissioned for the New Hampshire State House in Concord.) French is the renowned sculptor who produced the massive statue of Abraham Lincoln inside the Lincoln Memorial.

The absence of statues outside in the Yard was deliberate, as it was determined that one statue would place undue importance on one naval leader over another, setting a precedent and justifying the placement of many more.[51] It is unclear as to why the Lejeune statue was allowed.

By contrast, busts of naval and historical luminaries abound in public places in the Yard (many in the Museum are inaccessible during its extensive renovations, 2007–9):

- Bronze heroic bust of Commo. John Barry by Patrick A. O'Connor, 1949, located in the Museum;

- Bronze bust of Rear Adm. Richard E. Byrd Jr., Antarctic explorer, by Benjamin T. Gilbert, twentieth century, located in the Museum;

- Wooden heroic bust of Benjamin Franklin that once was the figurehead of USS *Franklin,* by William Rush, located in the Museum;

- Bronze heroic bust of Rear Adm. Albert Gleaves by Belle Kinney, 1938, located on the seaward balcony of Memorial Hall (in Bancroft Hall);

- Bronze bust of Adm. Henry Kent Hewitt, World War II commander of the 8th Fleet in the Mediterranean, by Wheeler Williams, located in the Museum;

- Marble, plaster, and bronze busts of Capt. John Paul Jones by Jean-Antoine Houdon, 1780, located in the Museum and as part of the display encircling Jones' sarcophagus in the crypt below the Chapel (see description of the Jones crypt on p. 24);

- Bronze miniature bust of President Abraham Lincoln, by Cravaua, nineteenth century, found bolted to a desk at the Naval Station Olongapo in the Philippines during the Spanish-American War, located in the Museum;

- Bronze bust of Adm. Ben Moreell, "Father of the Seabees," by Felix de Weldon, who also designed the Seabee Memorial at the entrance to Arlington National Cemetery, located at the Seabee monument on the seaward side of the Levy Center;

- Bronze, miniature statue of Adm. Horatio Lord Nelson, Royal Navy, by F. Brook Hitch, 1946, located in the Museum;

- Two busts of Fleet Adm. Chester Nimitz: bronze, heroic bust by Felix de Weldon, 1948, located in the Nimitz library; and fiberglass bust by John B. Weaver, 1965, located in the Museum;

The original bronze bust of John Paul Jones, sculpted by Jean-Antoine Houdon. *Courtesy Special Collections & Archives Division, Nimitz Library, U.S. Naval Academy.*

- Marble bust of Adm. David Dixon Porter by Franklin Simmons, 1876, located in the Museum;
- Bronze bust of Adm. Hyman G. Rickover by Paul D. Wegner, 1980, located in Rickover Hall;
- Bronze bust of John L. Senior, noted authority on John Paul Jones who collected and donated many Jones memorabilia to the Museum, by Paul Manship, 1947, located in the Museum;
- Wooden heroic bust of Tamanend, Chief of the Delaware Indians that was the figurehead of USS *Delaware,* by William Luke, 1836, located in the Visitor Center (bronze copy holds court in Tecumseh Court in front of Bancroft Hall);
- Wooden heroic bust of Alexander the Great that was the figurehead of HMS *Macedonian,* by unknown British sculptor, 1810, located on Stribling Walk near Mahan Hall; also called the *Macedonian* Monument;
- Bronze bust of President George Washington, by James W. A. MacDonald, 1898, modeled after the bust by Jean-Antoine Houdon;

Bust of Adm. Hyman G.
Rickover. *Courtesy Jamie
Howren Photography.*

- Wooden heroic bust of Gen. George Washington that
  was the figurehead of USS *Washington,* by Solomon
  Willard, 1816, located in the Museum. Willard was the
  designer of the Bunker Hill monument.

NAMESAKE WALKS, ROADS,
AND FIELDS IN THE YARD

More than thirteen miles of roads wind around the Yard
and fifteen miles of walkways traverse the Yard,[52] all
predominantly named for former superintendents, with
a handful honoring famous naval leaders or Academy
advocates.

The scenery in the Yard—of downtown Annapolis,
of the Severn River, and of the buildings of the Naval
Academy—has changed over the course of the school's
history, but many of the circuitous pathways and walks
were preserved when Flagg erected his "modern" plan
for the Academy. He simply "superimposed a cross axis

of paved arteries on the existing green space,"[53] to accommodate both individual strolling and marching battalions, with strategic intersections to provide the most ideal vistas of the French Renaissance buildings and the expanse of open water that formed the final side of the square. It also reminded visitors of the Academy's purpose.[54]

- Badger Road, named for Rear Adm. Charles J. Badger, Class of 1873, and former superintendent;
- Bailey Road, named for Maj. Kenneth D. Bailey, USMC, killed in action during the Battle of Guadalcanal and Medal of Honor recipient;
- Balch Road, named for Rear Adm. George B. Balch, former superintendent;
- Beardall Road, named for Rear Adm. John R. Beardall, Class of 1908, and former superintendent;
- Blake Road, named for Capt. George S. Blake, former superintendent who recommended the Naval Academy be transferred to Newport, Rhode Island, during the Civil War;
- Boone Walk, named for Adm. Walter F. Boone, Class of 1921, and former superintendent;
- Bowyer Road, named for Rear Adm. John M. Bowyer, Class of 1874, and former superintendent;
- Brownson Road, named for Capt. Williard H. Brownson, Class of 1865, and former superintendent;
- Buchanan Road, named for Capt. Franklin Buchanan, the first superintendent of the Naval Academy and for whom Buchanan House (the official residence of the superintendent) is named;
- Chambers Walk, named for Capt. Washington I. Chambers, Class of 1876, and a naval aviation pioneer;
- Cochrane Court, named for Vice Adm. Edward L. Cochrane, Class of 1914, famous naval architect and engineer;

- Cooper Road, named for Capt. Philip H. Cooper, Class of 1864, and former superintendent;
- Cushing Road, named for Cdr. William B. Cushing, Class of 1861 (not a graduate) and Civil War hero, who is buried in the Cemetery;
- Davidson Walk, named for Rear Adm. John F. Davidson, Class of 1929, and former superintendent;
- Decatur Road, named for the famous War of 1812 hero, Commo. Stephen Decatur, Jr., who is also memorialized at the Tripoli Monument behind Preble Hall;
- Dewey Field, named for Rear Adm. George Dewey, Class of 1858, the victor at the Battle of Manila Bay;
- Eberle Road, named for Adm. Edward W. Eberle, Class of 1885, and former superintendent;
- Ericsson Court, named for John Ericsson, Swedish-American inventor of the screw propeller and the naval architect of the USS *Monitor;*
- Farragut Field, named for Adm. David Glasgow Farragut, who was a naval hero of the Civil War and whose heroism in the Battle of Mobile Bay is depicted in a stained-glass window in the Chapel;
- Fullam Court, named for Capt. William F. Fullam, Class of 1877 and former superintendent;
- Gibbons Walk, named for Capt. John H. Gibbons, Class of 1879 and former superintendent;
- Griffin Court, named for Rear Adm. Robert S. Griffin, Class of 1878, and former chief of the Bureau of Engineering during World War I;
- Holloway Road, named for Adm. James L. Holloway Jr., Class of 1919, and former superintendent, whose son, Adm. James L. Holloway III, was a chief of naval operations;
- Ingram Field, named for Adm. Jonas H. Ingram, Class of 1907, who was awarded a Medal of Honor in 1914

and commanded the U.S. South Atlantic Fleet in
World War II;

- Turner Joy Road, named for Vice Adm. Charles
  Turner Joy, Class of 1916, and former superintendent;
- Longshaw Road, named for Assistant Surgeon William
  Longshaw Jr., killed in action in the Battle of Fort
  Fisher in the Civil War;
- McCandless Road, named for Rear Adm. Bruce
  McCandless, Class of 1932, and Medal of Honor recip-
  ient for his actions during the Battle of Guadalcanal in
  World War II;
- McNair Road, named for Rear Adm. Frederick V.
  McNair, Class of 1857, and former superintendent;
- Melson Walk, named for Vice Adm. Charles L.
  Melson, Class of 1927, and former superintendent;
- Rip Miller Field, named for Edgar E. "Rip" Miller,
  longtime and beloved football coach and athletic
  director at the Naval Academy in 1931–74;
- Moffett Walk, named for Rear Adm. William A.
  Moffett, Class of 1890, Medal of Honor recipient and
  former superintendent;
- Moreell Plaza, named for Adm. Ben Moreell, father
  of the Seabees;
- Osborne Road, named for Surgeon Weeden S.
  Osborne, who was killed in action during the Battle
  of Chateau Thierry in World War I and was awarded
  a Medal of Honor;
- Parker Road, named for Commo. Foxhall A. Parker,
  who died while serving as superintendent in 1879;
- Phythian Road, named for Capt. Robert L. Phythian,
  Class of 1856, and former superintendent;
- Porter Road, named for Rear Adm. David Dixon
  Porter, former superintendent;
- Powers Road, named for Lt. John J. Powers, Class of
  1935, who was killed in action during the Battle of

Coral Sea in World War II and earned a Medal
of Honor;

- Radford Terrace, named for Adm. Arthur W. Radford,
  Class of 1916, and chairman of the Joint Chiefs of Staff
  1953–57;
- Ramsey Road, named for Capt. Francis M. Ramsay,
  Class of 1856, and the first superintendent who was
  also an alumnus;
- Robison Road, named for Adm. Samuel B. Robison,
  Class of 1888, and former superintendent;
- Rodgers Road, named for Rear Adm. Christopher R.
  P. Rodgers, former superintendent who held the posi-
  tion twice (1874–78 and 1881);
- Sands Road, named for Rear Adm. James H. Sands,
  Class of 1864, and former superintendent;
- Santee Road, named after training ship USS *Santee,*
  which was moored at the Yard 1861–1912;
- Scales Road, named for Rear Adm. Archibald H.
  Scales, Class of 1887, and former superintendent;
- Forrest Sherman Field, named for Adm. Forrest P.
  Sherman, Class of 1918, former chief of
  naval operations;
- Sigsbee Way, named for Rear Adm. Charles D.
  Sigsbee, Class of 1864 and captain of the USS *Maine*
  when it was blown up in the Havana Harbor in 1898
  (the foremast of which is along the Sea Wall);
- Sims Road, named for Rear Adm. William S. Sims,
  Class of 1880, who commanded all U.S. naval forces
  during World War I;
- Smedberg Walk, named for Vice Adm. William
  R. Smedberg III, Class of 1926, and former
  superintendent;
- Soley Walk, named after James Russell Soley, Assistant
  Secretary of the Navy (1890–93), who wrote the
  History of the Naval Academy in 1876;

- Stribling Walk, named for Cdr. Cornelius K. Stribling, former superintendent;
- Thomas Walk, named for Rear Adm. William N. Thomas, a longtime Naval Academy chaplain, Navy chief of chaplains, and the author of "The Prayer of a Midshipman";
- Truxtun Road, named for Commodore Thomas Truxtun, legendary commander of the USS *Constellation* (1797–1800);
- Turner Field, named for Adm. Richmond K. Turner, Class of 1908, who commanded the Third Amphibious Force during World War II;
- Upshur Road, named after Cdr. George P. Upshur, the second superintendent at the Naval Academy, succeeding Buchanan;
- Wainwright Road, named for Rear Adm. Richard Wainwright, Class of 1868, and former superintendent;
- Henry B. Wilson Road, named for Adm. Henry B. Wilson, Class of 1881, and former superintendent;
- Wood Road, named for Medical Director William M. Wood, fleet surgeon in the Mexican and Civil Wars and former chief of the bureau of medicine and surgery;
- Worden Field, named after Rear Adm. John L. Worden, commander of the USS *Monitor* during the Civil War.

PART IV *Outside the yard*

Outside the yard

If you have time and want to visit some historical sites related to the Yard but outside the Yard, you might want to visit the Naval Academy Alumni House (or Ogle Hall) and the Navy-Marine Corps Memorial Stadium (best seen during a football game!). And while the Naval Academy Dairy (1902–98) is no longer open to the public, its storied history is covered here.

ALUMNI HOUSE
Two blocks from Gate Three, at the corner of King George Street and College Avenue, sits a classic Georgian home, built in 1739 and later occupied by Maryland Governor Samuel Ogle from 1747 until 1752. His son, Benjamin, also a governor, lived in the house as well, during which time he entertained George Washington in 1773.

The house was purchased by the Naval Academy Alumni Association in 1944 and since then has been used as its offices and gathering place. The house is meticulously maintained with periodic antiques, including a Hepplewhite sideboard—originally owned by the first secretary of the navy—decorating the entrance foyer and many portraits and painting of famous naval figures (including Buchanan).[55] The adjoining house is called "The 49 House," a Queen Anne–style building that was built in 1887 and so named because of its address: 49 College Avenue. It was purchased by the Alumni Association in 1983 and renovated to serve as office space, but many of its original details were kept intact, including a stairway with a carved-spindle balustrade and stained-glass windows on the landing.

While neither building is open to the public for tours, a virtual tour of Ogle Hall is available online at www.usna. com (click on events). Alumni Association members can rent rooms (and gardens) for business and social events by contacting the events coordinator at 410-295-4020.

NAVY–MARINE CORPS MEMORIAL STADIUM
The earliest football games at the Naval Academy in the 1880s were probably played on an old parade field. From the 1890s, the games were played on Worden Field until 1924, when they were moved to a new stadium on the seaward end of Dahlgren Hall, on land now occupied by Lejeune and Ricketts halls. All intercollegiate athletic events were played here, renamed Thompson Field in 1931, in honor of Col. Robert Means Thompson, co-founder of both the Naval Academy Alumni Association and the Athletic Association. As the Academy grew in students and stature, the antiquated stadium was deemed inadequate and a campaign was led under the direction of then-Superintendent Rear Adm. William R. Smedberg III, Class of 1926, and then-Capt. Eugene Fluckey, member of the Class of 1935 and Medal of Honor recipient from World War II.

They raised $2.2 million from private and state donors (a flag from every state in the Union flies above the stadium) and the new Navy-Marine Corps Memorial Stadium was dedicated on 26 September 1959, to all "who have served, and will serve, their country with honor, distinction and loyalty in the Navy and Marine Corps." It received a $41 million renovation in 2004 and can now

DID YOU KNOW?
The 1984 Olympic Games' soccer matches and the 2005 NCAA Women's Lacrosse Final Four matches were held in the Navy–Marine Corps Memorial Stadium.

hold 34,000 spectators, attracting crowds from all over the country for its football and lacrosse games. Outdoor graduation ceremonies have been held there since 1966.

For information on Navy sporting events, call 1-800-US-4-NAVY, or go to http://navysports.csdtv.com.

THE (FORMER) NAVAL ACADEMY DAIRY

In 1911, after an outbreak of typhoid fever at the Academy was linked to spoiled milk, Congress authorized the establishment of a dairy dedicated to provide the Brigade of Midshipmen its own supply of milk, cream, butter, and ice cream. A herd of 321 Holsteins provided fresh dairy products daily from an 875-acre farm in nearby Gambrills, Maryland, for more than eighty years. In 1998, the Academy determined that a larger, commercial supplier could provide the same services at a lower cost.

DID YOU KNOW?
The Naval Academy mascot, "Bill" the goat, is kept and cared for on the farm; a bronze statue of him is located at the corner of Porter and Cooper roads. For more on Bill, see p.104.

PART V *The best of the yard*

TOP FIVE CHILDREN'S ATTRACTIONS
*If you are visiting the Yard with young children
(or children at heart!), you might want to try these
attractions first:*

- Bill the Goat, p. 104;
- Gallery of ships in the U.S. Naval Academy Museum, p. 40;
- Static displays of Vietnam-era planes, p. 149;
- Tecumseh, the figurehead of the USS *Delaware,* p. 58;
- Visitor Center, p. 3.

TOP FIVE ARCHITECTURAL ATTRACTIONS
*If building styles intrigue you and your time in the Yard is
limited, visit these structures first:*

- Bancroft Hall, p. 70
- Chapel, p. 15
- Levy Center, p. 123
- Mahan Hall, p. 46
- Robert Crown Sailing Center, p. 120

BEST PLACES TO REST IN THE YARD
*If you are looking for a quiet place in the Yard to reflect or just
to enjoy the scenery, try these spots:*

- Benches near the Fitch Foot Bridge that crosses College Creek, p. 167
- Benches outside the Visitor Center, p. 3
- Chapel or Levy Center, p. 15 or p. 123
- Tecumseh Court, p. 65
- Zimmerman Bandstand, p. 9

Notes

1. Jack Sweetman and Thomas J. Cutler, *The Naval Academy: An Illustrated History,* 2nd ed. (Annapolis, Md.: United States Naval Institute, 1995), 10.

2. James Russell Soley, *Historical Sketch of the United States Naval Academy* (Washington, D.C.: Government Printing Office, 1876), 124–25.

3. Walter B. Norris, *Annapolis: Its Colonial and Naval Story* (New York: Thomas Y. Crowell Company Publishers, 1935), 246.

4. Neal Kitt, Project Manager & Architectural Designer, CSD Architects, telephone conversation with author, 14 April 2006.

5. Vicki Heath Escudé, "The United States Naval Academy: History of Homes and Anecdotes of Residents," 1994, 9.

6. Mardges Bacon, *Beaux-Arts Architect and Urban Reformer* (Cambridge, Mass.: The MIT Press, 1986), 112.

7. Ernest Flagg, "The New Naval Academy," U.S. Naval Institute's *Proceedings,* Vol. XXV, No. 4, December 1899, 866.

8. Bacon, *Beaux-Arts Architect,* 133.

9. Bacon, *Beaux-Arts Architect,* 130.

10. Bacon, *Beaux-Arts Architect,* 123.

11. Bacon, *Beaux-Arts Architect,* 131.

12. http://www.usna.edu/Chaplains/weddings.htm

13. Susan Stamberg, "California Dreamin'," Morning Edition, National Public Radio, 8 July 2002.

14. U.S. Naval Academy Museum, *Currier and Ives Navy: Lithographs from the Beverley R. Robinson Collection* (Annapolis, Md.: U.S. Naval Academy Museum, 1983), 1.

15. John Wilson, personal interview by author, Annapolis, Md., 29 December 2005.

16. Charles Belknap, "Catalogue of the Flags in the Naval Institute Hall" (Annapolis, Md.: U.S. Naval Academy, 1888), 14.

17. Naval Facilities Engineering Command, Department of the Navy, "Monument Survey: Legacy Project 878" (Annapolis, Md.: U.S. Naval Academy, 1995), 5.

18. Kendall Banning, *Annapolis Today* (New York and London: Funk & Wagnalls Company, 1938), 80–81.

19. Banning, *Annapolis Today,* 80.

20. Naval Facilities Engineering Command, "Monument Survey," 697.

21. Emil D. Di Motta Jr., "Legend of the Virgin Cannons," *Shipmate,* December 2004, 31.

22. Bacon, *Beaux-Arts Architect,* 123.

23. Naval Facilities Engineering Command, "Monument Survey," 704.

24. Banning, *Annapolis Today,* 253.

25. Ginger Doyel, "The U.S. Naval Academy's Second Renaissance, Part I: Bancroft Hall and its Center Section, 1901–1906," *Shipmate* (July–August, 2003), 27.

26. This is actually a replica of the original Perry flag, which underwent extensive renovation and preservation in 2005 and is now permanently housed in Preble Hall, away from sunlight and humidity.

27. Bacon, *Beaux-Arts Architect,* 127.

28. Elmer Martin Jackson Jr., *Annapolis* (Annapolis, Md.: n.p., 1936–37), 134.

29. Jackson, *Annapolis,* 132.

30. P. T. Deutermann, *Darkside* (New York: St. Martin's Press, 2002), 109. Reprinted with permission by the author.

31. Bacon, *Beaux-Arts Architect,* 121.

32. Banning, *Annapolis Today,* 182.

33. Banning, *Annapolis Today,* 185.

34. Neal Kitt, Project Manager and Architectural Designer, CSD Architects, telephone conversation with author, 13 April 2006.

35. James Webb, *A Sense of Honor* (Englewood Cliffs, N.J.: Prentice-Hall, Inc., 1981), 10–11. Reprinted with permission by the author.

36. Robert W. McNitt, *Sailing at the U.S. Naval Academy* (Annapolis, Md.: United States Naval Institute, 1996), 35.

37. Edsall, *A Place Called The Yard,* 21.

38. Tom Spies, Principal Architect, CSD Architects, telephone conversation with author, 11 April 2006.

39. Banning, *Annapolis Today,* 134.

40. Moreell Commission, "Report of the Special Advisory Commission on Future Developments of Academic Facilities for the United States Naval Academy" (Annapolis, Md.: U.S. Naval Academy, 1961), 19.

41. Historic Annapolis, Inc., "Three Ancient Blocks" (Annapolis, Md.: Historic Annapolis, Inc., 1963), 1.

42. "Academy's Plan For Expansion Stirs Annapolis," The *Baltimore Sun,* 11 March 1962, 40.

43. John Carl Warnecke, "Formal Façades For Annapolis," *Architectural Record,* June 1965, 157.

44. The main auditorium is named The Bob Hope Performing Arts Center, in honor of the late Mr. Hope's many years of support and entertainment of soldiers and sailors deployed overseas.

45. Sweetman and Cutler, *The Naval Academy,* 260.

46. Tami Terella, "House tour conjures up Naval Academy memories," *U.S. Naval Academy Trident,* 19 March 1993, 4.

47. Doyel, "The U.S. Naval Academy's Second Renaissance, Part I," 213–16.

48. H. C. Washburn, *Illustrated Case Inscriptions from the Official Catalogue of the Trophy Flags of the United States Navy* (Annapolis, Md.: The Lord Baltimore Press, 1913), 2.

49. Mary Daniels, "Seeing Stars," *Chicago Tribune,* 27 February 2005, 6.

50. Naval Facilities Engineering Command, "Monument Survey," 7.

51. Naval Facilities Engineering Command, "Monument Survey," 9.

52. Linda Foster and Roger Miller, *United States Naval Academy: Annapolis* (Baltimore, Md.: Image Publishing, Ltd., 2001), 13.

53. Bacon, *Beaux-Arts Architect,* 119.

54. Naval Facilities Engineering Command, "Monument Survey," 7.

55. Ginger Doyel, *Annapolis Vignettes* (Centreville, Md.: Tidewater Publishers, 2005), 197.

Index

About the authors

TAYLOR BALDWIN KILAND is the Vice President of Marketing and Communications at the United States Navy Memorial in Washington, D.C. She holds a master's degree from Northwestern University's Medill School of Journalism and a bachelor's degree in journalism from the University of Southern California. A former naval officer—the third generation in her family to serve, she has also worked as an account director for the global communications firm Burson-Marsteller, volunteered for numerous national political campaigns—including that of Senator John McCain's in 2000, and she continues to serve on several charitable boards of directors. Taylor is also the co-author of *Open Doors: Vietnam POWs Thirty Years Later* (Potomac Books, 2005)—a book about the current lives of 30 former POWs, and *The U.S. Navy and Military Careers* (Enslow Publishers, 2006)—a children's book about careers in the Navy. She lives in Arlington, Virginia.

Born in Washington, D.C., JAMIE HOWREN grew up in Alexandria, Virginia. She earned a bachelor of arts degree with a concentration in photography from Meredith College for Women of Raleigh, North Carolina, in 1989. Photographer and creator of the exhibit and book *Open Doors: Vietnam POWs Thirty Years Later,* she works as a free-lance photographer in Orange County, California, while raising her nine-year-old daughter.

The Naval Institute Press is the book-publishing arm of the U.S. Naval Institute, a private, nonprofit, membership society for sea service professionals and others who share an interest in naval and maritime affairs. Established in 1873 at the U.S. Naval Academy in Annapolis, Maryland, where its offices remain today, the Naval Institute has members worldwide.

Members of the Naval Institute support the education programs of the society and receive the influential monthly magazine *Proceedings* and discounts on fine nautical prints and on ship and aircraft photos. They also have access to the transcripts of the Institute's Oral History Program and get discounted admission to any of the Institute-sponsored seminars offered around the country. Discounts are also available to the colorful bimonthly magazine *Naval History*.

The Naval Institute's book-publishing program, begun in 1898 with basic guides to naval practices, has broadened its scope to include books of more general interest. Now the Naval Institute Press publishes about seventy titles each year, ranging from how-to books on boating and navigation to battle histories, biographies, ship and aircraft guides, and novels. Institute members receive significant discounts on the Press's more than eight hundred books in print.

Full-time students are eligible for special half-price membership rates. Life memberships are also available.

For a free catalog describing Naval Institute Press books currently available, and for further information about subscribing to *Naval History* magazine or about joining the U.S. Naval Institute, please write to:

Member Services
U.S. Naval Institute
291 Wood Road
Annapolis, MD 21402-5034
Telephone: (800) 233-8764
Fax: (410) 571-1703
Web address: www.navalinstitute.org